INSTANT INFORMATION ON THE INTERNET!

A Genealogist's No-Frills Guide to ꜱ̲ᴛʜᴇ BRITISH ISLES

CHRISTINA K. SCHAEFER

D1104271

GENEALOGICAL PUBLISHING Co. Inc.

Published by Genealogical Publishing Co., Inc.
1001 N. Calvert St., Baltimore, Md. 21202
Library of Congress Catalogue Card Number 99-71540
International Standard Book Number 0-8063-1614-4
Made in the United States of America

❧ CONTENTS

iii

❧ INTRODUCTION

The second volume in the *Instant Information on the Internet!* series, this is a no-frills guide to the most important genealogy sites in Great Britain and Ireland. It tells how and where to locate records, contact other researchers, exchange information, and locate indexes that can be searched free of charge on a home computer. Designed specifically for speed and convenience, this second volume of *Instant Information on the Internet!* provides immediate access to the top tier of British and Irish genealogy resources on the Internet and is the logical starting point for genealogical research in this promising new medium.

Instant Information on the Internet! is organized by country, and thereunder by county. Under each county are listed, in the following order (as applicable):

1. The record office or facility that holds official records such as local authority archives (boroughs, rural districts, urban districts, etc.), larger public archives, and parish and Non-conformist archives.
2. Libraries, museums, societies, and other resources (in alphabetical order).
3. A section of information sites listing how-to information, local history sources, and so forth.
4. A selection of indexes (some as lists, some in databases), documents, maps, and publications in digitized form.
5. Sites containing links to other sites, and lists of addresses of important genealogical resources.

The agencies responsible for maintaining, archiving, and preserving original records are similar in function but can vary greatly in name. In England, Scotland, and Wales, archives of local authorities may be found in combined facilities with a library, under the title of "Local Studies Collection" or "Local History Collection." In Ireland, Heritage Centres have been established in the counties to assist with genealogical and local history research.

In addition to the sections containing important Internet addresses for England, Scotland, Wales, and Ireland, four other sections are located in the book as follows: (1) the web sites for The Church of England are found immediately after the "England" section, and (2) The (Anglican) Church in Wales follows "Wales." The third and fourth sections are at the end of the book: one is devoted to resources on Celtic languages and Celtic history which may be found online, and the other explains the County Archive Research Network (CARN).

As a dedicated bibliophile, I favor published guides to accompany any research endeavor so I can plan in advance what needs to be done and the order in which I want to do it. With the fast and furious pace of cyber information, it is still a good idea to leave a paper trail. *Instant Information on the Internet!* helps pinpoint in advance not only where information can be found on the Internet, but how to backtrack and reconstruct what has already been searched.

Abbreviations and Acronyms Used

The following are found throughout this book:

CARN	County Archive Research Network
GENUKI	The UK and Ireland Genealogical Information Service
GRO	General Register Office (Scotland)
IGI	International Genealogical Index
OPAC	Online Public Access Catalogue
FHS	Family History Society
PRO	Public Record Office
PRONI	Public Record Office of Northern Ireland
UK	United Kingdom

Additionally, the symbol ✳ indicates a site with links to other sites.

Other Internet Resources

One of the greatest advantages to genealogical research online is the accessibility of other researchers through mailing lists, interest groups, chat rooms, message boards, etc. The list is quite extensive, and the following links cover most of these online sites:

✳ Cyndi's List of UK and Ireland Mailing Lists, Newsgroups, and Chat
http://www.cyndislist.com/genuk.htm#Mailing

✳ Cyndi's List of UK and Ireland Queries, Message Boards, and
    Surname Lists
http://www.cyndislist.com/genuk.htm#Queries

✳ Genealogy Mailing Lists
http://www.genuki.org.uk/indexes/MailingLists.html#MON
> This page provides genealogy-related mailing lists for those with research interests in areas of the British Isles, including England, Wales, Scotland, Ireland, the Channel Islands, and the Isle of Man.

Look-up Lists

Look-up lists are made up of volunteers who are willing to search for specific entries, usually in books they own. To ask for a look-up, click on the name next to the reference. Requests should be specific, giving as many details as possible. It is best to avoid asking for time-consuming research; also, if a volunteer is willing to obtain copies of the relevant pages, it is expected that expenses will be reimbursed.

✳ England Look-up Exchange
http://freespace.virgin.net/m.harbach/england.html

✳ Wales Look-up Exchange
http://freespace.virgin.net/m.harbach/wales/lookupw.html

✳ Scotland Look-up Exchange
http://www.geocities.com/Heartland/Acres/6317/sct.htm

✳ Isle of Man Look-up Exchange
http://www.isle-of-man.com/interests/genealogy/look-up.htm

✳ Genealogy Helplist Ireland
http://www.geocities.com/Athens/Delphi/4715/genealog/helpireland.html

✳ Channel Islands Volunteers/Lookups
http://members.aol.com/johnf14246/ci/volunteers.html

GEOGRAPHIC ORGANIZATION

The British Isles is a geographic term used to describe the two large islands of Great Britain (England, Scotland, and Wales) and Ireland, including smaller islands adjacent to their coasts. Following a geographic standard, I have grouped entries under England, Wales, Scotland, the Isle of Man, the Channel Islands, and Ireland (Northern Ireland and the Republic of Ireland). The name United Kingdom or "UK" is a political one, having evolved as follows:

- 1707—*United Kingdom of Great Britain* (union of the Parliaments of England and Scotland)
- 1801—*United Kingdom of Great Britain and Ireland* (when Ireland joined the Union)
- 1922—*United Kingdom of Great Britain and Northern Ireland* (when the Irish Free State, the forerunner of the Republic of Ireland, was formed from twenty-six of the thirty-two counties of Ireland)

In a nutshell: British local government has been based upon town charters for local self government (from the twelfth century, known as free burghs in Scotland) and the ecclesiastical parish (from the seventeenth century). In the 1830s, government reform increased local responsibility for policing, highways, and the provision of public utilities. County councils were set up in 1889 and then abolished in 1902–3 in England and Wales (1918 in Scotland), and replaced with a less-complex structure of authorities organized in a smaller number of tiers. This structure was reworked in the Local Government Act 1972 (Scotland and Northern Ireland in 1973).

For administrative purposes, the largest units of local government became county councils (regional councils in Scotland). In 1985 the Local Government Act abolished the administrative county councils in England (1996 in Scotland) in favor of a single-tier structure of unitary authorities (at the same time retaining the boundaries of the historic counties). Within the geographical area they covered were a number of district councils, except for Greater London and the six English metropolitan counties where there has been a single tier of unitary authorities since 1985. In some parts of England and Wales there are parish councils (community councils in Wales) below the level of the district councils.

Additionally, there are four island communities in the United Kingdom: the Isle of Wight in England, and the Orkney Islands, the Shetland Islands, and the Western Isles (now called Comhairle nan Eilean Siar) in Scotland, each having their own island councils. This does not include the Channel

Islands and the Isle of Man, which are dependencies of the British Crown and have their own Parliaments.

Further reform in 1991 (1994 in Scotland) led the government to lean toward single-tier authorities to "be much better placed to build strong links with all interests in its local community."[1] The resulting reorganization is as follows:

- *England*: thirty-four county councils and forty-six unitary authorities as of 1 April 1998.
- *Wales*: twenty-two unitary authorities as of 1 April 1996.
- *Scotland*: twenty-nine unitary authorities (plus three island councils) as of 1 April 1996.
- *London Boroughs and Metropolitan Districts*: thirty-two London boroughs and the City of London, and thirty-six metropolitan districts as of 1 April 1996.

What Does This Mean for Genealogy?

"The new county boundaries are administrative areas, and will not alter the traditional boundaries of counties, nor is it intended that the loyalties of people living in them will change despite the different names adopted by the new administrative counties."—government statement quoted in *The Times*, 1 April 1974

Beginning in 1974, the administrative county boundary changes have resulted in an archival nightmare. For example, the historic county of Lancashire is now divided among the unitary authorities of Greater Manchester, Merseyside, and the counties of Lancashire and Cheshire. Some records have remained in their traditional record offices while others have been moved to new facilities. There are also groups of years, both pre- and post-1974, where records are split between two archives.

The changes put into effect in 1974 abolished only the administrative counties and regions created in 1889. The ancient geographical counties were left alone; however, many people began referring to the new administrative counties and regions instead of the historic geographic ones. The Family History Library (FHL) of The Church of Jesus Christ of Latter-day Saints and the Society of Genealogists (SOG) in London use the historic counties to catalog county, town, and parish records. With the exception of the county of Monmouthshire (which the FHL has under England and I have put under Wales), I have continued this approach.

---

[1] "The Structure of Local Government in Scotland: Shaping the New Councils," Scottish Office, October 1992, p. 7.

My goal has been to ascertain where information about records can be found online. To do this, I referred to lists of local authorities, pre-1974, 1974 to 1996, and the current status. To alleviate what I have come to refer to as the mysteries of "geography roulette," I have included the following lists here in the introduction. The three-letter abbreviations are the Chapman Codes for the counties.

ENGLAND *ENG*
Counties in England, Pre-1974
Bedfordshire *BDF*
Berkshire *BRK*
Buckinghamshire *BKM*
Cambridgeshire *CAM*
Cheshire *CHS*
Cornwall *CON*
Cumberland *CUL*
Derbyshire *DBY*
Devon *DEV*
Dorset *DOR*
Durham *DUR*
Essex *ESS*
Gloucestershire *GLS*
Hampshire *HAM*
Herefordshire *HEF*
Hertfordshire *HRT*
Huntingdonshire *HUN*
Kent *KEN*
Lancashire *LAN*
Leicestershire *LEI*
Lincolnshire *LIN*
London (city only) *LND*
Middlesex *MDX*
Norfolk *NFK*
Northamptonshire *NTH*
Northumberland *NBL*
Nottinghamshire *NTT*
Oxfordshire *OXF*
Rutland *RUT*
Shropshire (Salop) *SAL*
Somerset *SOM*
Staffordshire *STS*
Suffolk *SFK*
Surrey *SRY*
Sussex *SSX*

Warwickshire *WAR*
Westmorland *WES*
Wiltshire *WIL*
Worcestershire *WOR*
Yorkshire *YKS*
YKS (East Riding) *ERY*
YKS (North Riding) *NRY*
YKS (West Riding) *WRY*

Counties in England, 1974–1986/1996–8
Avon (Gloucestershire [part], Somerset [part]) *AVN*
Bedfordshire (Bedfordshire) *BDF*
Berkshire (Berkshire [part], Buckinghamshire [part]) *BRK*
Buckinghamshire (Buckinghamshire [part]) *BKM*
Cambridgeshire (Cambridgeshire, Huntingdonshire) *CAM*
Cheshire (Cheshire [part], Lancashire [part]) *CHS*
Cleveland (Durham [part], North Riding [part]) *CLV*
Cornwall (Cornwall) *CON*
Cumbria (Cumberland, Lancashire [part], Westmorland, West Riding [part]) *CMA*
Derbyshire (Derbyshire, Cheshire [part]) *DBY*
Devon (Devon) *DEV*
Dorset (Dorset, Hampshire [part]) *DOR*
Durham (Durham [part], North Riding [part]) *DUR*
East Sussex (Sussex [part]) *SXE*
Essex (Essex [part]) *ESS*
Gloucestershire (Gloucestershire [part]) *GLS*

Greater London (London, Essex
[part], Hertfordshire [part], Kent
[part], Middlesex, Surrey [part])
LND

Greater Manchester (Cheshire [part],
Lancashire [part], West Riding
[part]) *GTM*

Hampshire (Hampshire [part]) *HAM*

Hereford and Worcester
(Herefordshire, Worcestershire
[part]) *HWR*

Hertfordshire (Hertfordshire [part])
HRT

Humberside (East Riding [part],
Lincolnshire [part], West Riding
[part]) *HUM*

Isle of Wight (Hampshire [part]) *IOW*

Kent (Kent [part]) *KEN*

Lancashire (Lancashire [part], West
Riding [part]) *LAN*

Leicestershire (Leicestershire,
Rutland) *LEI*

Lincolnshire (Lincolnshire [part]) *LIN*

Merseyside (Cheshire [part],
Lancashire [part]) *MSY*

Norfolk (Norfolk, Suffolk [part]) *NFK*

Northamptonshire
(Northamptonshire) *NBL*

Northumberland (Northumberland
[part]) *NTH*

North Yorkshire (East Riding [part],
North Riding [part], West Riding
[part]) *NYK*

Nottinghamshire (Nottinghamshire
[part]) *NTT*

Oxfordshire (Oxford, Berkshire
[part]) *OXF*

Shropshire (Shropshire) *SAL*

Somerset (Somerset [part]) *SOM*

South Yorkshire (Nottinghamshire
[part], West Riding [part]) *SYK*

Staffordshire (Staffordshire [part])
STS

Suffolk (Suffolk [part]) *SFK*

Surrey (Surrey [part]) *SRY*

Tyne & Wear (Durham [part],
Northumberland [part]) *TWR*

Warwick (Warwickshire [part]) *WAR*

West Midlands (Staffordshire [part],
Warwickshire [part],
Worcestershire [part]) *WMD*

West Sussex (Sussex [part], Surrey
[part]) *SXW*

West Yorkshire (West Riding [part])
WYK

Wiltshire (Wiltshire) *WIL*

County Councils in England as of 1998

Bedfordshire
Buckinghamshire
Cambridgeshire
Cheshire
Cornwall
Cumbria
Derbyshire
Devon
Dorset
Durham
East Sussex
Essex
Gloucestershire
Hampshire
Hertfordshire
Kent
Lancashire
Leicestershire
Lincolnshire
Norfolk
Northamptonshire
Northumberland
North Yorkshire
Nottinghamshire
Oxfordshire
Shropshire
Somerset
Staffordshire
Suffolk
Surrey
Warwickshire
West Sussex
Wiltshire
Worcestershire

Unitary Authorities in England as of 1998 (independent of the county councils)

Arun District Council
Bath and North East Somerset Council
Blackburn Borough Council
Blackpool Borough Council
Bournemouth Borough Council
Bracknell Forest District Council
Brighton and Hove Council
Bristol City Council
Darlington Borough Council
Derby City Council
East Yorkshire Borough Council
Halton Borough Council
Hartlepool Council
Herefordshire Council
Isle of Wight County Council
Kingston-upon-Hull City Council
Leicester City Council
Luton Borough Council
Medway Towns
Middlesbrough Borough Council
Milton Keynes Borough Council
Newbury District Council
North-East Lincolnshire Council
North Lincolnshire Council
North Somerset Council
Nottingham City Council
Peterborough City Council
Plymouth City Council
Poole Borough Council
Portsmouth City Council
Reading Borough Council
Redcar and Cleveland Borough Council
Rutland District Council
Slough Borough Council
South Gloucestershire Council
Southampton City Council
Southend-on-Sea Borough Council
Stockton-on-Tees Borough Council
Swindon Borough Council
Telford and Wrekin Council
Thurrock District Council
Torbay Borough Council
Warrington Borough Council
Windsor and Maidenhead Royal Borough Council
Wokingham District Council
York City Council

Geographical Areas in England as of 1996 (not political divisions)

Greater Manchester
Merseyside (includes the boroughs of Knowsley, Liverpool, St. Helens, Sefton, and Wirral)
Tyne & Wear
West Midlands

Councils in England as of 1998

Greater London

WALES *WLS*
Counties in Wales, Pre-1974
Anglesey *AGY*
Breconshire *BRE*
Caernarfonshire *CAE*
Cardiganshire *CGN*
Carmarthenshire *CMN*
Denbighshire *DEN*
Flintshire *FLN*
Glamorganshire *GLA*
Merionethshire *MER*
Monmouthshire *MON*
Montgomeryshire *MGY*
Pembrokeshire *PEM*
Radnorshire *RAD*

Counties in Wales, 1974–1996

Clwyd (Denbighshire [part], Flintshire, Merionethshire [part]) *CWD*
Dyfed (Cardiganshire, Carmarthenshire, Pembrokeshire) *DFD*

Gwent (Breconshire [part], Monmouthshire) *GNT*
Gwynedd (Anglesey, Caernarfonshire, Denbighshire [part], Merionethshire [part]) *GWN*
Mid Glamorgan (Glamorganshire [part], Breconshire [part]) *MGM*
Powys (Brecon [part], Montgomeryshire, Radnorshire) *POW*
South Glamorgan (Glamorganshire [part]) *SGM*
West Glamorgan (Glamorganshire [part]) *WGM*

Counties in Wales as of 1996
Anglesey
Carmarthenshire
Ceredigion (Cardiganshire)
Denbighshire
Flintshire
Glamorgan
Gwynedd
Monmouthshire (Gwent)
Pembrokeshire
Powys
West Glamorgan
Wrexham

SCOTLAND *SCT*
Counties in Scotland, Pre-1974
Aberdeenshire *ABD*
Angus (Fofar) *ANS*
Argyllshire *ARL*
Ayrshire *AYR*
Banffshire *BAN*
Berwickshire *BEW*
Buteshire *BUT*
Caithness-shire *CAI*
Clackmannanshire *CLK*
Dumbartonshire *DNB*
Dumfriesshire *DFS*
East Lothian *ELN*
Fifeshire *FIF*

Inverness-shire *INV*
Kincardineshire *KCD*
Kinross-shire *KRS*
Kirkcudbrightshire *KKD*
Lanarkshire *LKS*
Midlothian *MLN*
Morayshire *MOR*
Nairnshire *NAI*
Orkney *OKI*
Peeblesshire *PEE*
Perthshire *PER*
Renfrewshire *RFW*
Ross & Cromarty *ROC*
Roxburghshire *ROX*
Selkirkshire *SEL*
Shetland *SHI*
Stirlingshire *STI*
Sutherland *SUT*
West Lothian *WLN*
Wigtownshire *WIG*

Regions in Scotland, 1974–1996
Borders (Berwickshire, Midlothian [part], Peeblesshire, Roxburghshire, Selkirkshire) *BOR*
Central (Clackmannanshire, Perthshire [part], Stirlingshire, West Lothian [part]) *CEN*
Dumfries and Galloway (Dumfriesshire, Kirkcudbright-shire, Wigtownshire) *DGY*
Fife (Fife) *FIF*
Grampian (Aberdeenshire, Banffshire, Kincardineshire, Morayshire) *GMP*
Highland (Argyllshire [part], Caithness-shire, Inverness-shire, Morayshire [part], Nairnshire, Ross & Cromarty [part], Sutherland) *HLD*
Lothian (East Lothian, Midlothian [part], West Lothian [part]) *LTN*
Orkney *OKI*
Shetland *SHI*

Strathclyde (Argyllshire [part], Ayrshire, Buteshire, Dunbartonshire, Lanarkshire, Renfrewshire, Stirlingshire [part]) *STD*

Tayside (Angus, Kinross-shire, Perthshire [part]) *TAY*

Western Isles (Inverness-shire [part], Ross & Cromarty [part]) *WIS*

Unitary Authorities in Scotland as of 1996

Aberdeen City
Aberdeenshire
Angus
Argyll and Bute
Clackmannanshire
Dumbarton and Clydebank
Dumfries and Galloway
Dundee City
East Ayrshire
East Dunbartonshire
East Lothian
East Renfrewshire
Edinburgh City
Eilean Siar, Comhairle nan (formerly Western Isles)
Falkirk
Fife
Glasgow City
Highland
Inverclyde
Midlothian
Morayshire
North Ayrshire
North Lanarkshire
Orkney Islands
Perthshire and Kinross
Renfrewshire
The Scottish Borders
Shetland Islands
South Ayrshire
South Lanarkshire
Stirlingshire
West Dunbartonshire
West Lothian

THE ISLE OF MAN
(dependency of the British Crown) *IOM*

THE CHANNEL ISLANDS
(dependency of the British Crown) *CHI*
Alderney *ALD*
Guernsey *GSY*
Jersey *JSY*
Sark *SRK*

NORTHERN IRELAND
(part of the United Kingdom) *IRL*
Counties in Northern Ireland
Antrim *ANT*
Armagh *ARM*
Down *DOW*
Fermanagh *FER*
Londonderry (Derry) *LDY*
Tyrone *TYR*

THE REPUBLIC OF IRELAND *IRL*
Counties in the Republic of Ireland
Carlow *CAR*
Cavan *CAV*
Clare *CLA*
Cork *COR*
Donegal *DON*
Dublin *DUB*
Galway *GAL*
Kerry *KER*
Kildare *KID*
Kilkenny *KIK*
Laois (Queens) *LEX*
Leitrim *LET*
Limerick *LIM*
Longford *LOG*
Louth *LOU*
Mayo *MAY*
Meath *MEA*
Monaghan *MOG*

Offaly (Kings) *OFF*

Roscommon *ROS*

Sligo *SLI*

Tipperary *TIP*

Waterford *WAT*

Westmeath *WEM*

Wexford *WEX*

Wicklow *WIC*

BRITISH ISLES: BASIC INFORMATION

These are the three most important sites for conducting genealogical research in the British Isles.

⁎ ARCHON (Archives Online)
http://www.hmc.gov.uk/archon/archon.htm

ARCHON is the principal information gateway for UK archivists and users of manuscript sources for British history. It is hosted and maintained by the Royal Commission on Historical Manuscripts. ARCHON accesses information on all repositories in the UK and throughout the world which have collections of manuscripts which are noted on the British National Register of Archives.

⁎ Royal Commission on Historical Documents,
  Manorial Documents Register
http://www.hmc.gov.uk/mdr/mdr.htm

Manorial Documents Register (MDR) is maintained by this Commission, on behalf of the Master of the Rolls, as a record of the whereabouts of manorial documents in England and Wales. Manorial records survive today in many national and local record offices and in some cases in private hands. The Commission itself holds no manorial records. Although the majority of the MDR is not computerized, the sections relating to Wales and Yorkshire are computerized and are available online.

⁎ The UK & Ireland Genealogical Information Service (GENUKI)
  Home Page
http://www.genuki.org.uk/

ENGLAND

This section also includes UK-wide resources, which will not be repeated under Wales, Scotland, Ireland, or the islands. Facilities with a national focus are listed here, rather than under the counties where they are physically located.

INSTANT INFORMATION ON THE INTERNET!

The Family Records Centre, London
http://www.pro.gov.uk/about/frc/default.htm
> Holds civil registration (births, deaths, and marriages), non-parochial parish registers, and miscellaneous returns of foreign births, deaths, and marriages. Available on microform are the following: census enumerations, Estate Duty Office death registers, Prerogative Court of Canterbury wills, and more.

Public Record Office (PRO), Kew, Richmond, Surrey
http://www.pro.gov.uk/
> The PRO is a national archive, holding all official records except those at the Family Records Centre. Some of the most important genealogical records include Chancery proceedings, Close Rolls, Hearth Tax returns, military and naval records, apprenticeship records (Board of Stamps), and various classes of records relating to property and inheritance.

The British Library, London
http://www.bl.uk/index.html

The British Library Oriental and India Office Collections, London
http://www.bl.uk/collections/oriental/records/iorfamhi.html

The College of Arms, London
http://www.kwtelecom.com/heraldry/collarms/

Commonwealth War Graves Commission, Maidenhead
http://www.cwgc.org/cwgchome.htm

The Federation of Family History Societies
http://members.aol.com/gfhsoc/

Guildhall Library, Manuscripts Collection, London
http://ihr.sas.ac.uk/ihr/ghmnu.html

Imperial War Museum, London
http://www.iwm.org.uk/

National Maritime Museum, Greenwich, London
http://www.nmm.ac.uk/

Post Office Archives, London
http://www.cs.ncl.ac.uk/genuki/PostOffice/

Royal Armouries Museum (Leeds, London, and Fort Nelson, Portsmouth)
http://www.armouries.org.uk/

The Society of Genealogists, London
http://www.sog.org.uk/index.html

INFORMATION SITES

"Battles Fought in England, Scotland, and Wales," by Peter R. Hamilton-Leggett
http://www.argonet.co.uk/users/hamleg/bat.html

Births, Deaths, and Marriages Overseas (from Great Britain)
http://ihr.sas.ac.uk/ihr/ghinfo6.html#births

✳ British Family History in India
http://www.ozemail.com.au/~clday/

British Genealogy Abbreviations and Acronyms
http://www.gendocs.demon.co.uk/abbr.html

The British Monarchy Official Web Site
http://www.royal.gov.uk/index.htm

Census and Related Materials
http://www.staffs.ac.uk/schools/humanities_and_soc_sciences/census/stdshome.htm
   Includes downloadable printed maps, Poor Law Union registration districts, etc.

Certificates of Births, Marriages, and Deaths
http://www.ons.gov.uk/services/cert.htm

Church Net UK Genealogy Information
http://churchnet.ucsm.ac.uk/genealogy/

Complete Alphabetical Index of Records Information Leaflets from the PRO
http://www.pro.gov.uk/leaflets/riindex.htm

Family History Research at the Imperial War Museum
http://www.iwm.org.uk/famhist.htm

✻ Family History Society Catalogs On-line
http://www.geocities.com/Heartland/Plains/8555/fhspubs.html

Genealogy Before the Parish Registers
http://www.pro.gov.uk/leaflets/ri028.htm

Legal Terms in Land Records
http://www.ultranet.com/~deeds/legal.htm

The National Pub and Brewery History Web Site
http://www.btinternet.com/~steven.williams1/pubpg intro.htm
National Pub Database for England through 1920, history of old English inns, etc.

✻ National Register of Archives, London
http://www.hmc.gov.uk/nra/nra.htm

Organisations Involved in the Immigration of Females
http://dcs1.uwaterloo.ca/~marj/genealogy/women.html

PRO Bookshop Online
http://www.pro.gov.uk/bookshop/default.htm

Ranks, Professions, Occupations, and Trades
http://www.gendocs.demon.co.uk/trades.html

Ron Taylor's UK 1851 Census Finding Aids and Indexes
http://rontay.digiweb.com/

UK Registration Districts
http://www.users.zetnet.co.uk/blangston/genuki/reg/

SELECTED DOCUMENTS AND INDEXES ONLINE

A–Z of British Genealogical Research, by Dr Ashton Emery (1996)
http://www.genuki.org.uk/big/EmeryPaper.html
Guide to researching British ancestry: the IGI, using parish registers, the civil registration system, the nineteenth-century census returns, archives, indexes and sources, etc.

Britain's Victorian Navy and Army in Old Photographs
http://www.tech.plymouth.ac.uk/swest/plymouth/history/def.htm

Debt of Honour Register
http://yard.ccta.gov.uk/cwgc/register.nsf
> This Register provides personal and service details and places of commemoration for the 1.7 million members of the Commonwealth forces who died in the First or Second World Wars, and death dates of some 60,000 civilian casualties.

Directory of Royal Genealogical Data
http://www.dcs.hull.ac.uk/public/genealogy/royal/catalog.
 html#BritishIsles

England Tombstone Project (transcriptions)
http://www.rootsweb.com/~engcemet/

Harvard Law School Library Catalogue of Medieval and Early Modern Deeds of England and Wales (arranged by county)
http://www.law.harvard.edu/library/guides/deeds/county.html

Immigrant Ships Transcribers Guild: English Ports
http://istg.rootsweb.com/departures/england.html
> Ports of Bristol, Cowes (Isle of Wight), Deal, Gravesend, Hull, Liverpool, London, Plymouth, and Southampton.

Internet Library of Early Journals: A Digital Library of Eighteenth- and Nineteenth-Century Journals
http://www.bodley.ox.ac.uk/ilej/

The Local Historian: Contents Pages and Abstracts of Articles
http://www.le.ac.uk/hi/LOCAL_HISTORY/

Map of the Counties of England, Scotland, and Wales Prior to the 1974 Boundary Changes
http://www.genuki.org.uk/big/BRITAIN2.GIF

Ordnance Survey: Gazetteer of Place Names for the UK
http://www.campus.bt.com/CampusWorld/pub/OS/Gazetteer/
 index.html

People Finder: United Kingdom
http://www.192.com/search.htm

✷ UK Interactive Map
http://www.uktravel.com/ukmap.html

✳ UK Standard Geographic Base (UKSGB)
http://www.ngdf.org.uk/uksgb/homepage.htm
> The UKSGB provides users and suppliers of geographic information with a standard and consistent approach to commonly used geographic units in the UK. Those currently included in the UKSGB are the administrative and postal jurisdictions.

LISTS AND LINKS

✳ Church Net UK Links to UK Churches
http://churchnet.ucsm.ac.uk/ukchurches/

✳ Directory of UK Local Government on the Web
http://www.tagish.co.uk/tagish/links/localgov.htm
> Includes all unitary, county, district, and borough authority-badged sites currently available.

✳ England GenWeb Project
http://www.rootsweb.com/~engwgw/index.html

✳ Familia: Family History Resources in Public Libraries in Britain and Ireland
http://www.earl.org.uk/familia/

Family History Centers in the British Isles
http://www.lds.org/en/2_How_Do_I_Begin/Where_is_Locations/ 11_British_Isles.html

✳ Local History Magazine Links for Local Historians
http://www.local-history.co.uk/links.html

✳ NISS (National Information Services and Systems)
http://www.niss.ac.uk/reference/index.html
> NISS service pages provide access to a wide variety of reference, bibliographic and directory material, including collections containing library OPACs (Online Public Access Catalogues) in higher education, bookshops and publishers, other library resources, reference works, network directories, museums and galleries, search engines, etc.

✳ North of England Regional Information Service
http://ris.niaa.org.uk/

✳ UK Archival Repositories on the Internet
http://www.archivesinfo.net/uksites.html

⅏ BEDFORDSHIRE

Bedford Central Library, Local Studies Library, Bedford
http://www.earl.org.uk/familia/services/bedfordshire.html

Bedford Museum, Bedford
http://www.museums.co.uk/bed/

Bedfordshire FHS, Bedford
http://www.bfhs.org.uk/

Luton Museum and Art Gallery, Luton
http://www.luton.gov.uk/museums.htm

INFORMATION SITES

Civil Registration Districts in Bedfordshire
http://www.users.zetnet.co.uk/blangston/genuki/reg/bdf.htm

LISTS AND LINKS

* Bedfordshire GENUKI Home Page
http://www.blunham.demon.co.uk/genuki/BDF/

List of All the Town and Parish Clerks for Mid Bedfordshire
http://www.midbeds.gov.uk/ycul.htm

⅏ BERKSHIRE

In 1974 Berkshire lost the Vale of the White Horse including Abingdon, Didcot, Wantage, and Wallingford, to Oxfordshire, but gained Slough from Buckinghamshire. An earlier boundary change assimilated Reading's growth north of Thames into Berkshire. In 1998 the administrative county was divided into six unitary authorities, based on the existing districts of Bracknell, Newbury, Reading, Slough, Windsor and Maidenhead, and Wokingham.

Berkshire Record Office, Reading
No Internet presence at this time, will be established in 2000
Berkshire County Council was abolished in April 1997, but the Berkshire Record Office continues, supported by all six new Unitary Authorities. The Record Office is planning to relocate to a new record office, probably in 2000, to be built in Reading. The archives will remain intact.

Berkshire FHS Research Centre, Reading
http://www.vellum.demon.co.uk/genuki/BRK/berksfhs/berks-rc.htm

Berkshire Local History Association, Reading
http://www.vellum.demon.co.uk/genuki/BRK/berkslha/index.htm

Berkshire Record Society, Reading
http://www.vellum.demon.co.uk/genuki/BRK/berksrs/index.htm

Reading Central Library, Berkshire County Local Studies Library,
    Reading
http://dspace.dial.pipex.com/town/street/ae556/
    The library has the largest collection of printed material about the town
    of Reading and Berkshire County in existence.

The Rural History Centre, University of Reading, Reading
http://www.reading.ac.uk/Instits/im/home.html

SELECTED DOCUMENTS AND INDEXES ONLINE

Map of Berkshire, 1801
http://www.library.yale.edu/MapColl/bkshire.htm

LISTS AND LINKS

❋ Berkshire GENUKI Home Page
http://www.genuki.org.uk/big/eng/BRK/

❧ BUCKINGHAMSHIRE

Buckinghamshire County Library Local Studies Section, Aylesbury
http://www.earl.org.uk/earlweb/special/scbucks.html

Buckinghamshire FHS
http://www.bucksfhs.org.uk/

INFORMATION SITES

The Buckinghamshire Hundreds and Their Parishes
http://met.open.ac.uk/genuki/big/eng/BKM/hundreds.html

Buckinghamshire Libraries with Family History Resources
http://www.earl.org.uk/familia/services/buckinghamshire.html

Civil Registration Districts in Buckinghamshire
http://www.users.zetnet.co.uk/blangston/genuki/reg/bkm.htm

SELECTED DOCUMENTS AND INDEXES ONLINE

Buckinghamshire FHS Databases
http://www.bucksfhs.org.uk/dindex1.htm

Alphabetical Surname Index to *Robson's 1839 Directory of Buckinghamshire*, by David Kolle, Names A–F
http://met.open.ac.uk/genuki/big/eng/BKM/directories/bucksdira.txt

Robson's 1839 Directory, Names G–O
http://met.open.ac.uk/genuki/big/eng/BKM/directories/bucksdirg.txt

Robson's 1839 Directory, Names P–Y
http://met.open.ac.uk/genuki/big/eng/BKM/directories/bucksdirp.txt

LISTS AND LINKS

✳ Buckinghamshire GENUKI Home Page
http://met.open.ac.uk/genuki/big/eng/BKM/

❧ CAMBRIDGESHIRE

In 1974 Cambridge absorbed the County of Huntingdon and City of Peterborough. Local government is vested in the Cambridgeshire County Council, Cambridge City Council, East Cambridgeshire District Council, Fenland District Council, Huntingdonshire District Council, Peterborough City Council, and South Cambridgeshire District Council.

Cambridge Central Library, Cambridgeshire Collection, Cambridge
http://www.camcnty.gov.uk/library/lib1/cambs.htm

Cambridge University Library, Ely Diocesan Records
http://www.lib.cam.ac.uk/MSS/Edr.html

Peterborough Central Library, Local Studies Collection, Peterborough
http://www.earl.org.uk/familia/services/cambs_peterborough.html

Wisbech District Library, Wisbech
http://www.earl.org.uk/familia/services/cambs_wisbech.html

INFORMATION SITES

* Cambridgeshire Local History Page
http://www.demon.co.uk/ecoln/lhist.html

Historic Places in Cambridge
http://www.camcnty.gov.uk/sub/visit/hp.htm

History of Haddenham
http://dspace.dial.pipex.com/town/place/fm27/history.htm

SELECTED DOCUMENTS AND INDEXES ONLINE

Contemporary Map of Cambridgeshire
http://www.camcnty.gov.uk/sub/visit/cambmap.htm

LISTS AND LINKS

* Cambridgeshire GENUKI Home Page
http://www.genuki.org.uk/big/eng/CAM/

* Cambridgeshire Town and Village Web Sites
http://www.camcnty.gov.uk/sub/local.htm

ᔒ CHESHIRE (see also Lancashire)

The boundaries of Cheshire were altered in 1974 with the formation of the new counties of Greater Manchester and Merseyside. The Trafford District of Cheshire became part of Greater Manchester County (with Bolton, Bury, Manchester, Oldham, and Rochdale from Lancashire). Wirral became part of Merseyside County (with Knowsley, Liverpool, St. Helens, and Sefton from Lancashire).

Cheshire Record Office, Chester
http://www.cheshire.gov.uk/recoff/home.htm

Chester Archives, Chester
http://www.chestercc.gov.uk/heritage/archives/home.html

Chester City Record Office
http://www.chestercc.gov.uk/chestercc/htmls/archives.htm

Tameside Archives, Local Studies Library, Stalybridge
http://dspace.dial.pipex.com/town/street/xlx81/index.htm
> Local authority including Turnpike Trust (Saltersbrook); public archives; religious archives including Non-conformist; Manchester Regiment Archives, etc.

Trafford Local Studies Centre, Sale
http://www.earl.org.uk/familia/services/trafford.html

Wirral Metropolitan Borough Archives Service, Birkenhead Central Library, Birkenhead
http://www.wirral.gov.uk/library/index.htm
> Local authority archives from the late eighteenth century, public archives, etc.

INFORMATION SITES

Wirral Past and Present
http://www.wirral.gov.uk/wirlpast.htm

SELECTED DOCUMENTS AND INDEXES ONLINE

Index to Wills at the Cheshire Record Office, 1492–1857
http://www.users.zetnet.co.uk/blangston/chswills

LISTS AND LINKS

✳ Cheshire GENUKI Home Page
http://www.users.zetnet.co.uk/blangston/genuki/chs.htm

Index to Cheshire Parishes
www.users.zetnet.co.uk/blangston/genuki/chspars/

❧ CORNWALL

Cornwall County Record Office, Truro
http://www.cornwall-online.co.uk/cw/cro.htm

Cornish Studies Library, Redruth
http://www.earl.org.uk/familia/services/cornwall.html

Cornwall FHS
http://www.cfhs.demon.co.uk/Society/

The Courtney Library and Cornish History Archive, Truro
http://www.cornwall-online.co.uk/ric/Welcome.html

INFORMATION SITES

Cornish Parish Registers
http://www.cfhs.demon.co.uk/Society/churchrecs.html

SELECTED DOCUMENTS AND INDEXES ONLINE

The Cornish Mining Index
http://www.cfhs.demon.co.uk/mining_index.txt

Harvard Law School Deeds Project: Cornwall
http://www.law.harvard.edu/library/guides/deeds/cornwall.html

LISTS AND LINKS

✼ All Things Cornish Webrings
http://web.ukonline.co.uk/alan.richards/

✼ Cornwall GENUKI Home Page
http://www.cfhs.demon.co.uk/

✼ Cornwall Links
http://celt.net/og/angcorn.htm

❧ CUMBERLAND (CUMBRIA)

The counties of Cumberland and Westmorland, the Furness district of
Lancashire (Lonsdale north of the Sands), and the parishes of Dent,
Garsdale, and Sedbergh in the former West Riding of Yorkshire were
formed into the administrative county of Cumbria in 1974. Records from
these areas can be found in the offices of the Cumbria Archive Service
at Carlisle, Kendal, Barrow-in-Furness, and Whitehaven. Records relating to the north and east of the historic county of Cumberland are in the
Carlisle office. The Record Office and Local Studies Library in Whitehaven
houses records relating to places south and west of the River Derwent
and north of the River Duddon. Records relating to the former county of
Westmorland and the Sedbergh district are in Kendal. Records relating
to Furness are in the Barrow office.

Cumbria Archive Service
http://www.magicnet.net/~noble/genuki/culcro.html

Carlisle Library, Carlisle
http://www.earl.org.uk/familia/services/cumbria_carlisle.html

Cumbria Record Office and Local Studies Library, Whitehaven
http://www.earl.org.uk/familia/services/cumbria_whitehaven.html

Workington Library, Workington
http://www.earl.org.uk/familia/services/cumbria_workington.html

LISTS AND LINKS

❋ Cumberland GENUKI Home Page
http://www.genuki.org.uk/big/eng/CUL/

❧ DERBYSHIRE

Chesterfield Library, Chesterfield
http://www.earl.org.uk/familia/services/derbys_chesterfield.html

Derby Local Studies Library, Derby
http://www.earl.org.uk/familia/services/derbys_city.html

Matlock Local Studies Library, Libraries and Heritage Department,
   Matlock
http://www.earl.org.uk/familia/services/derbys_mat.html

LISTS AND LINKS

❋ Derbyshire GENUKI Home Page
http://www.homeusers.prestel.co.uk/renfrew/genuki/DBY/

North East Derbyshire Web Pages
http://www.geopages.com/Athens/1992/ned.html

❧ DEVON

Devon Record Office
http://www.devon-cc.gov.uk/dro/
   This includes the Devon Record Office in Exeter, the North Devon Record
   Office in Barnstaple, and the Office and City of Plymouth and West Devon
   Record Office in Plymouth.

City of Plymouth Central Local Studies Library
http://www.plymouth.gov.uk/star/library.htm

City of Plymouth Central Library, Naval Studies Collection
http://www.plymouth.gov.uk/star/library.htm

North Devon Local Studies Centre, Barnstaple
http://www.devon-cc.gov.uk/library/locstudy/barnstap.html

Plymouth Naval Base Museum, Devonport, Plymouth
http://www.cronab.demon.co.uk/pnbm3.htm

Torquay Local Studies Library, Torquay
http://www.devon-cc.gov.uk/library/locstudy/torquay.html

University of Exeter Library, Special Collections, Exeter
http://www.exeter.ac.uk/~ijtilsed/lib/guides/specoll.html

Westcountry Studies Library, Devon Studies Centre, Exeter
http://www.devon-cc.gov.uk/library/locstudy/wsl.html

INFORMATION SITES

✳ Devon Local Studies Service Home Page
http://www.devon-cc.gov.uk/library/locstudy/homepage.html

History of Walkhampton Village
http://www.argonet.co.uk/users/hamleg

Roger Meyrick's Peter Tavy Page
http://dspace.dial.pipex.com/town/terrace/xds53/

LISTS AND LINKS

✳ Devon GENUKI Home Page
http://www.cs.ncl.ac.uk/genuki/DEV/

❧ DORSET

Dorset Record Office, Dorchester
http://www.dorset-cc.gov.uk/records.htm

Dorset Reference Library, Dorchester
http://www.dorset-cc.gov.uk/dorcol.htm

LISTS AND LINKS

✳ Dorsetshire GENUKI Home Page
http://www.genuki.org.uk/big/eng/DOR/

❧ DURHAM (see also Northumberland)

Durham Record Office, Durham
http://www.durham.gov.uk/alm/rec.htm

Tyne & Wear Archives Service, Newcastle-upon-Tyne
http://ris.niaa.org.uk/archives/

Darlington Library, Centre for Local Studies, Darlington
http://www.earl.org.uk/familia/services/darlington.html

Durham City Library, Reference and Local Studies Department
http://www.earl.org.uk/familia/services/durham.html

Gateshead Libraries Local Studies Collection, Gateshead
http://www.gatesheadmbc.gov.uk/libraries/localst.htm
Serves the Gateshead Metropolitan Borough area, and, secondarily, the counties of Durham, Northumberland, and Tyne & Wear.

South Tyneside Central Library, Local History Library, South Shields
http://ris.niaa.org.uk/heritage-north/stl/hist.htm
Serves the towns of South Shields, Hebburn, and Jarrow.

Stockton Reference Library, Stockton-on-Tees
http://www.earl.org.uk/familia/services/stockton.html

University of Durham Library: Archives and Special Collections
http://www.dur.ac.uk/Library/asc/index.html

INFORMATION SITES

County Durham History
http://ourworld.compuserve.com/homepages/north_east_england_
history_page/COUNTYDURHAM.htm

County Durham Remembers the Great War
http://www.durham.gov.uk/dli/dli_home.htm

Surnames of North Eastern England
http://ourworld.compuserve.com/homepages/north_east_england_history_page/SURNAMES.htm

Transcripts and Indexes at the Tyne & Wear Archives Service
http://ris.niaa.org.uk/archives/11_Transcripts.html

University of Durham Library, Archives and Special Collections List
http://www.dur.ac.uk/Library/asc/navidocs/content1.html#C01

SELECTED DOCUMENTS AND INDEXES ONLINE

❊ Seaham Super Index
http://dspace.dial.pipex.com/town/street/kch66/

Genealogical and local history database for Easington District (Castle Eden, Cold Hesledon, Dalton-le-Dale, Deaf Hill, Easington Village, Haswell, Hawthorn, Hulam, Hutton Henry, Monk Hesleden, Murton, Nesbitt, Seaham, Seaton, Sheraton, Shotton, South Hetton, South Wingate, Station Town, Thornley, Wheatley Hill, and Wingate) in the county of Durham.

LISTS AND LINKS

❊ Durham GENUKI Home Page
http://homepages.enterprise.net/pjoiner/genuki/DUR/

❧ ESSEX

Essex Record Office, Chelmsford
http://www.essexcc.gov.uk/heritage/fs_recof.htm

University of Essex, Albert Sloman Library Special Collections, Chelmsford
http://libwww.essex.ac.uk/guide/speccol.html

SELECTED DOCUMENTS AND INDEXES ONLINE

Map of a Farm in the Parish of Great Burstead, Near Billericay, 1699
http://www.rsl.ox.ac.uk/nnj/webmapsf.htm

LISTS AND LINKS

✳ Essex GENUKI Home Page
http://privatewww.essex.ac.uk/~esfh/genuki/

✳ Essex Libraries with Family History Resources
http://www.earl.org.uk/familia/services/essex.html

❧ GLOUCESTERSHIRE

Gloucestershire Record Office, Gloucester
http://www.gloscc.gov.uk/pubserv/gcc/corpserv/archives/index.htm

Bristol Record Office
http://www.bristol-city.gov.uk/cgi-bin/w3menu?A+BCS00600+BG+F+
AMM00101+AMM00203+BCS00103+BCS00505

Bristol Reference Library, Bristol
http://www.earl.org.uk/familia/services/bristol.html

✳ Fishponds Local History Society, Bristol
http://www.bunjie.freeserve.co.uk/

Gloucestershire Collection, County Library, Gloucester
http://www.earl.org.uk/familia/services/gloucester.html

Yate Library, Yate
http://www.earl.org.uk/familia/services/south_gloucs.html

LISTS AND LINKS

✳ Gloucestershire GENUKI Home Page
http://www.genuki.org.uk/big/eng/GLS/

❧ HAMPSHIRE

Hampshire Record Office, Winchester
http://www.hants.gov.uk/record-office/index.html

Bitterne Local History Society, Southampton
http://www.interalpha.net/customer/bitterne/

Portsmouth City Record Office and Museums
http://www.portsmouthcc.gov.uk/a.htm

Quaker FHS: Hampshire
http://www.qfhs.mcmail.com/counties/hants.htm

Southampton City Archives
http://www.southampton.gov.uk/Atoz/archive.htm

Southampton Special Collections Library, Southampton
http://www.southampton.gov.uk/Libraries/specialc.htm

University of Southampton Library Archive and Manuscript Collections
http://www.soton.ac.uk/~papers1/collections/wwwintro.html

INFORMATION SITES

Major Resources Available at the Hampshire Record Office
http://www.hants.gov.uk/record-office/sources.html

SELECTED DOCUMENTS AND INDEXES ONLINE

Map of Winchester, 1805
http://www.library.yale.edu/MapColl/winc1805.htm

LISTS AND LINKS

* Hampshire GENUKI Home Page
http://www.genuki.org.uk/big/eng/HAM/index.html

* Hampshire Libraries with Family History Resources
http://www.earl.org.uk/familia/services/hampshire.html

❧ HEREFORDSHIRE

In 1974 the former counties of Herefordshire and Worcestershire were combined to form Hereford and Worcester. It was then divided into nine districts: Bromsgrove, Leominster, Malvern Hills, Redditch, South Herefordshire, Wychavon, Wyre Forest, and the cities of Hereford and Worcester. In 1998 a new unitary authority for Herefordshire and a county council for Worcestershire replaced the administrative county of Hereford and Worcester. The new Herefordshire Council incorporates the former district councils of South Herefordshire, Leominster, and Hereford City.

Hereford Record Office
http://193.128.154.20/pages/h&w_cc/hfd_rec1.htm

INFORMATION SITES

❋ City of Hereford Web Pages
http://www.ibmpcug.co.uk/~mserve/hereford.html

LISTS AND LINKS

❋ Herefordshire GENUKI Home Page
http://www.genuki.org.uk/big/eng/HEF/

❋ Herefordshire Libraries with Family History Resources
http://www.earl.org.uk/familia/services/hereford.html

❧ HERTFORDSHIRE

Hertfordshire County Archives and Local Studies, Hertford
http://hertslib.hertscc.gov.uk/histindx.htm

Hertfordshire County Record Office, Hertford
http://www.hertscc.gov.uk/hcc/records/index.htm

Hertfordshire Family and Population History Society, St. Albans
http://www.btinternet.com/~hfphs/index.htm

Hertfordshire Record Society, Hitchin
http://hertslib.hertscc.gov.uk/recsocie.htm

INFORMATION SITES

A Brief History of Hertfordshire
http://www.hertscc.gov.uk/herts/history.htm

Discover Hertford
http://www.hertfordtown.co.uk/

Hertfordshire Archives and Local Studies: Discover Your Family History
http://hertslib.hertscc.gov.uk/famstart.htm

Hertfordshire County Record Office: Parish Registers
http://www.hertscc.gov.uk/hcc/records/coelist.htm

The History of Hertford Schools
http://www.hertfordtown.co.uk/histschool.htm

St. Albans' Genealogy in Hertfordshire
http://www.stalbans.gov.uk/

Watford History
http://walker.theresistance.net/watford/wathist.htm

LISTS AND LINKS

✳ Hertfordshire GENUKI Home Page
http://homepages.enterprise.net/pjoiner/genuki/HRT/

List of Hertfordshire Museums
http://hertslib.hertscc.gov.uk/locmusms.htm

❧ HUNTINGDONSHIRE (see also Cambridgeshire)

The County of Huntingdon and the City of Peterborough were absorbed into the administrative county of Cambridgeshire in 1974. Huntingdonshire is now a District Council of Cambridgeshire. Geographically, it still exists as a county.

Cambridgeshire County Record Office, Huntingdon
http://www.genuki.org.uk/big/eng/HUN/RecordOffice.html

Huntingdon Library, Huntingdonshire Collection, Huntingdon
http://www.earl.org.uk/familia/services/cambs_huntingdon.html

Huntingdonshire FHS
http://www.genuki.org.uk/big/eng/HUN/HFHS/

Huntingdonshire Society
http://www.rahbarnes.demon.co.uk/hunts.htm

Huntingdon Town Council Home Page
http://www.camcnty.gov.uk/partners/parish/huntstc/htchome.htm
> Huntingdon includes the villages of Alconburys, Fenstanton, the Hemingfords, and the Stukeleys and the towns of Godmanchester, Ramsey, St. Ives, and St. Neots.

INFORMATION SITES

Historic St. Ives
http://www.hlalapansi.demon.co.uk/StIves/index.html

Huntingdonshire: A Unique County of England
http://dspace.dial.pipex.com/town/estate/aao34

Quakers in Huntingdonshire
http://www.qfhs.mcmail.com/counties/hunts.htm

SELECTED DOCUMENTS AND INDEXES ONLINE

Map of Cambridgeshire with Huntingdonshire
http://www.camcnty.gov.uk/sub/visit/cambmap.htm

LISTS AND LINKS

✳ Cambridgeshire Town and Village Web Sites
http://www.camcnty.gov.uk/sub/local.htm

✳ Huntingdonshire GENUKI Home Page
http://www.genuki.org.uk/big/eng/HUN/

❧ ISLE OF WIGHT

> The island now forms a magisterial division of Hampshire. The Isle of Wight Council was created in 1995 as a unitary authority to replace the former Isle of Wight County Council and the two borough councils of Medina and South Wight.

Isle of Wight County Record Office, Newport
http://www.genuki.org.uk/big/eng/HAM/IOW/recoff.html

Isle of Wight FHS, Newport
http://www.dina.clara.net/iowfhs/

INFORMATION SITES

Churches on the Isle of Wight
http://www.wightonline.co.uk/

LISTS AND LINKS

✳ Isle of Wight GENUKI Home Page
http://www.genuki.org.uk/big/eng/HAM/IOW/

❧ KENT

Centre for Kentish Studies, Maidstone
http://www.earl.org.uk/familia/services/kent_maidstone.html

Broadstairs Library, Broadstairs
http://www.earl.org.uk/familia/services/kent_broadstairs.html

Canterbury Library, Canterbury
http://www.earl.org.uk/familia/services/kent_canterbury.html

Dartford Central Library Reference Department, Dartford
http://www.earl.org.uk/familia/services/kent_dartford.html

Dover Library, Dover
http://www.earl.org.uk/familia/services/kent_dover.html

Faversham Library, Faversham
http://www.earl.org.uk/familia/services/kent_faversham.html

Folkestone Library Heritage Room, Folkestone
http://www.earl.org.uk/familia/services/kent_folkestone.html

Gillingham Library, Gillingham
http://www.earl.org.uk/familia/services/kent_gillingham.html

Gravesend Library, Gravesend
http://www.earl.org.uk/familia/services/kent_gravesend.html

Herne Bay Library, Herne Bay
http://www.earl.org.uk/familia/services/kent_herne_bay.html

Kent FHS
http://www.centrenet.co.uk/~cna49/kfhs.htm

Margate Library, Margate
http://www.earl.org.uk/familia/services/kent_margate.html

Ramsgate Library and Museum, Ramsgate
http://www.earl.org.uk/familia/services/kent_ramsgate.html

Rochester-upon-Medway Studies Centre, Rochester
http://www.earl.org.uk/familia/services/kent_rochester.html

Sevenoaks Library, Sevenoaks
http://www.earl.org.uk/familia/services/kent_sevenoaks.html

Sheerness Library, Sheppey
http://www.earl.org.uk/familia/services/kent_sheerness.html

Sittingbourne Library, Sittingbourne
http://www.earl.org.uk/familia/services/kent_sittingbourne.html

Tunbridge Wells Library, Tunbridge Wells
http://www.earl.org.uk/familia/services/kent_tunbridge.html

Whitstable Library, Whitstable
http://www.earl.org.uk/familia/services/kent_whitstable.html

INFORMATION SITES

✳ Canterbury and Kent Genealogical Resources
http://www.digiserve.com/peter/index.htm

SELECTED DOCUMENTS AND INDEXES ONLINE

Pigot's Commercial Directory for Kent (1839)
http://users.ox.ac.uk/~malcolm/genuki/big/eng/KEN/picotken.txt

Ramsgate Registered Vessels, 1835–1844
http://www.kentnet.co.uk/kentinfo.htm

LISTS AND LINKS

✳ Kent GENUKI Home Page
http://users.ox.ac.uk/~malcolm/genuki/big/eng/KEN/resource.htm

❧ LANCASHIRE

Lancashire formerly included all or part of every city and metropolitan district in Greater Manchester. The boundaries of Lancashire were altered in 1974 with the formation of the new counties of Cumbria, Greater Manchester, and Merseyside. The counties of Cumberland and Westmorland, the Furness District of Lancashire (Lonsdale north of the Sands), and the parishes of Sedbergh, Garsdale, and Dent in the former West Riding of Yorkshire were formed into the administrative county of Cumbria. The south east became part of Greater Manchester County (Bolton, Bury, Manchester, Oldham, and Rochdale), along with the Trafford District of Cheshire. The south west became part of Merseyside County (currently Knowsley, Liverpool, St. Helens, and Sefton, and Wirral from Cheshire).

Lancashire Record Office, Local Studies Library, County Library
Headquarters, Preston
http://www.lancashire.com/lcc/edu/ro/index.htm

Local authority archives including Boroughs (Ashton-under-Lyne, Bury, Heywood, Middleton, Mossley, Prestwich, Radcliffe, Rochdale, and Stretford), Rural District (Barton-upon-Irwell), Urban Districts (Audenshaw, Chadderton, Crompton, Denton, Droylsden, Failsworth, Lees, Littleborough, Milnrow, Ramsbottom, Royton, Tottington, Turton, Urmston, Wardle, and Whitworth). Holds Poor Law Unions (Ashton-under-Lyne, Barton-upon-Irwell, Bury, Oldham, Rochdale); public archives including Quarter Sessions; probate (Chester Diocese, Lancashire south of the Ribble and including Saddleworth); and religious archives including the Manchester Diocese (tithe awards and bishops' transcripts, see also Manchester City Archives), Blackburn and Liverpool Dioceses (see also Liverpool City Record Office), and Methodist and other Non-conformist churches.

Greater Manchester County Record Office (GMCRO), Manchester
http://www.gmcro.u-net.com/

Local authority records for Bury and Trafford Districts (see also Bury Archive Service and Trafford Central Library), public records (Bolton, Bury, Manchester, Oldham, and Rochdale), valuation books (see also Manchester City Archives), etc. GMCRO holds no parish registers, either originals or copies (see Manchester City Archives). Greater Manchester County Record Office was opened in 1976, two years after the establishment of the metropolitan county councils in England and Wales. After the abolition of Greater Manchester County Council in 1986, the area came under the control of the Association of Greater Manchester Authorities. While it has been possible to transfer some types of records to these other offices, much material remains here (for the areas removed from the county in 1974) because it cannot be separated from the main series of records, e.g., wills and Quarter Sessions records.

Merseyside County Record Office, Central Library, Liverpool
http://www.liv.ac.uk/~archives/mersey2.htm#MRO
> Local authority and public archives; religious archives include Methodist and United Reform churches; estate archives, etc.

Bolton Archive and Local Studies Service, Central Library, Bolton
http://www.earl.org.uk/familia/services/bolton.html

Bury Central Library Reference and Information Services, Bury
http://www.earl.org.uk/familia/services/bury.html

Crosby Library, Waterloo, Liverpool
http://www.earl.org.uk/familia/services/sefton.html

Cunard Archives, University of Liverpool
http://www.liv.ac.uk/~archives/cunard/chome.htm

Knowsley Archives, Libraries and Local Studies Department, Huyton
http://www.knowsley.gov.uk/leisure/libraries/history/index.html
> Serves Cronton, Huyton, Kirkby, Knowsley, Prescot, Roby, Simonswood, Tarbock, and Whiston.

Liverpool City Record Office, Central Library and Local Studies
http://www.liverpool.gov.uk/public/council_info/direct-info/leisure/
> **libraries/ro.htm**
> Local authority archives from 1207; Poor Law Unions Board of Guardians minutes and records and workhouse records; religious archives including Anglican parishes from 1586, Roman Catholic parishes from 1741, Non-conformist from 1787, Liverpool Diocesan Registry (see also Lancashire Record Office), Jewish archives from 1804, etc. The Office also houses the library of the Historic Society of Lancashire and Cheshire.

Liverpool and South West Lancashire FHS
http://www.lswlfhs.freeserve.co.uk

Manchester City Archives Department, Central Library,
> Local Studies Unit
http://www.manchester.gov.uk/mccdlt/libguide/cenlib/frame.htm
> Public archives including Salford Hundred Court of Record, Manchester City Sessions and Petty Sessions, hospitals, valuation maps (see also Greater Manchester Record Office), and records of the Territorial Army; religious archives including the Manchester Diocese and Methodist and other Non-conformist churches, Jewish synagogues, etc.

Oldham Local Studies Library, Oldham
http://www.earl.org.uk/familia/services/oldham.html

Rochdale Local Studies Library, Arts and Heritage Centre, Rochdale
http://www.earl.org.uk/familia/services/rochdale.html

Sefton Metropolitan Borough Archives, Southport
http://www.liv.ac.uk/~archives/mersey2.htm#sEF
Holds some local authority records for pre-1974. The borough was formed in 1974, combining the areas of Bootle, Crosby, and Southport with parts of the West Lancashire district.

St. Helens Metropolitan Borough Local History and Archives,
    Central Library, St. Helens
http://www.liv.ac.uk/~archives/mersey2.htm#StH
Local authority archives from 1845–1980, Poor Law archives for the township of Parr, 1688–1828, etc. The Borough includes Billinge, Bold, Eccleston, Haydock, Newton-le-Willows, Rainford, and Rainhill.

University of Liverpool, Sydney Jones Library, Special Collections and
    Archives
http://www.liv.ac.uk/~archives/home.htm

University of Manchester, John Rylands Library, Methodist Archives and
    Research Centre
http://rylibweb.man.ac.uk/data1/dg/text/method.html

Wigan History Shop, Wigan
http://www.earl.org.uk/familia/services/wigan.html
Wigan local library collections and microforms of church registers formerly made available at Wigan Archives Service (in Leigh, Wigan: it holds local authority archives including Poor Law Unions and public archives including Quarter Sessions and Petty Sessions, but has **no Internet presence**).

INFORMATION SITES

✳ Archives on Merseyside: A Guide to Local Archive Services
http://www.liv.ac.uk/~archives/mersey2.htm

✳ Genealogy in Darwen and Blackburn
http://ourworld.compuserve.com/homepages/GAFOSTER

✳ Guide to Greater Manchester Repositories
http://www.gmcro.u-net.com/reposit.htm

Knowsley Local History: Its People and Heritage
http://history.knowsley.gov.uk/

✳ Lancashire County Museum Service
http://www.lancashire.com/lcc/edu/lb/musindx.htm

✳ Lancashire Local History Federation
http://www.local-history.co.uk/groups/Lancashire.html

SELECTED DOCUMENTS AND INDEXES ONLINE

Greater Manchester County Gazetteer, by Andrew Cross
http://www.gmcro.u-net.com/gazframe.htm

Lancashire Gazetteer, by Joseph Aston (1808)
http://www.genuki.org.uk/big/eng/LAN/Gazetteer/

The Pictorial History of the County of Lancaster (1854)
http://www.pcug.org.au/~pfthomps/lancshis/lancsint.htm

Pigot's and Slater's Topography of the British Isles: Warrington
**http://www.staffs.ac.uk/schools/humanities_and_soc_sciences/census/
    pigstart.htm**

Royal Lancashire Volunteers Index, Eighteenth Century
http://www.gmcro.u-net.com/militia/index.htm

LISTS AND LINKS

✳ Lancashire GENUKI Home Page
http://www.genuki.org.uk/big/eng/LAN/

❧ LEICESTERSHIRE

Leicestershire County Council Home Page
http://www.leics.gov.uk/lcc/council/departments.html
> The local government includes Charnwood Borough Council, Harborough
> District Council, North West Leicestershire District Council, and Oadby
> and Wigston Borough Council.

Leicester and Rutland FHS, Wigston
http://www.geocities.com/Heartland/Pointe/3446/index.html

INFORMATION SITES

Loughborough Local History
http://www.loughborough.com/COMMUNIT/comm5.htm

LISTS AND LINKS

✳ Leicestershire GENUKI Home Page
http://www.genuki.org.uk/big/eng/LEI/

❧ LINCOLNSHIRE

Lincolnshire Archives, Lincoln
http://www.lincs-archives.com/

North East Lincolnshire Central Library, Great Grimsby
http://www.earl.org.uk/familia/services/north_east_lincs.html

Scunthorpe Central Library, Scunthorpe
http://www.earl.org.uk/familia/services/north_lincs.html

SELECTED DOCUMENTS AND INDEXES ONLINE

Lincolnshire Archives Search Indexes and Scroll for Convicts, 1787–1840
http://www.demon.co.uk/lincs-archives/convicts.htm

Lincolnshire Poor Law Union Records, 1834–1930
http://www.lincs-archives.com/poor_law.pdf

Martin Smith's *History of Stamford*
http://www.stamford.co.uk/tourism/smithist.htm

LISTS AND LINKS

✳ Lincolnshire GENUKI Home Page
http://www.genuki.org.uk/big/eng/LIN/

✳ Lincolnshire Libraries with Family History Resources
http://www.earl.org.uk/familia/services/lincolns.html

❧ LONDON AND MIDDLESEX

In 1889 the boundaries of the City of London became one and the same with the newly created administrative county of London. Added to the new county were parts of Kent, Middlesex, and Surrey counties. This area was then divided into boroughs. Greater London replaced the county of London in 1963, and also absorbed the rest of Middlesex and parts of Essex and Hertfordshire as well as some county boroughs. The London boroughs were then reorganized. In addition to what is listed immediately following, see the general resources listed under "England" at the beginning of this section.

London Metropolitan Archives
http://www.cityoflondon.gov.uk/organisation/services/records.htm
Holdings concentrate on the archives of London institutions including parishes, hospitals, charities, and businesses as well as large estates and public utilities. It holds the archives of the Greater London Council, the London and Middlesex County Councils, and their predecessors.

The Corporation of London Records Office
http://www.cityoflondon.gov.uk/organisation/services/records.htm
Holdings comprise the official archives of the Corporation of London. These include charters and administrative records of the government of the city dating back to 1275, judicial and financial records of the city, architectural plans and drawings, and other schemes dating from the fifteenth century.

Guildhall, London
**http://www.cityoflondon.gov.uk/history/archiheritage/
    guildhallframed.htm**
The official repository for historical records relating to the City of London (except for those of the Corporation of London Records Office); holdings include printed works on all aspects of London history.

(London Borough of) Hackney Archives Department
http://www.hackney.gov.uk/archive/first1.htm

(London Borough of) Hammersmith and Fulham Libraries
http://www.lbhf.gov.uk/

(London Borough of) Wandsworth Local History Library, Battersea
    Library, Lavender Hill
http://www.earl.org.uk/partners/wandsworth/services.html#localhist

City of Westminster's Archive Center, London
http://www.gold.ac.uk/genuki/LND/Westminster/

East of London FHS
http://ourworld.compuserve.com/homepages/jordan/eolfhs.htm
> Serves the area of Greater London north of the Thames extending from the edge of the City of London at Bishopsgate and Aldgate, eastward through the London Boroughs of Hackney, Tower Hamlets, Newham, Redbridge, Barking, and Dagenham, to the edge of Metropolitan Essex at Havering.

London and North Middlesex FHS
http://www.lnmfhs.dircon.co.uk
> Serves the City of London, Marylebone, and the London Boroughs of Barnet, Camden, Enfield, Haringey, and Islington.

The Society of Genealogists, London
http://www.sog.org.uk/index.html

West Middlesex FHS
http://home.clara.net/dchilds/wmfhs/

INFORMATION SITES

✳ Eastside Community Heritage (East London)
http://www.eastside.ndirect.co.uk/

Parish Register Copies in the Library of the Society of Genealogists: City of London
http://www.sog.org.uk/prc/lnd.html

Searching London Marriage Licence Records
http://ihr.sas.ac.uk/ihr/ghinfo12.html#marriage

Searching London Probate Records
http://ihr.sas.ac.uk/ihr/ghinfo13.html#probate

Victorian London Research
http://www.gendocs.demon.co.uk/victorian.html#HOME

SELECTED DOCUMENTS AND INDEXES ONLINE

Greenwood's *Map of London* (1827)
http://www.bathspa.ac.uk/greenwood/home.html

The London Jews Database
http://www1.jewishgen.org/databases/londweb.htm

Maps of the London Area, 1666, 1830, and 1840
http://www.rsl.ox.ac.uk/nnj/webmapsf.htm

Middlesex Parish Records Database, 1563–1895
http://www.enol.com/~infobase/gen/parish/

LISTS AND LINKS

✳ London GENUKI Home Page
http://www.gold.ac.uk/genuki/LND/

✳ Middlesex GENUKI Home Page
http://www.gold.ac.uk/genuki/MDX/

❧ MONMOUTHSHIRE (see Wales)

❧ NORFOLK

Norfolk Record Office, Norwich
http://www.norfolk.gov.uk/council/departments/nro/nroindex.htm

✳ Great Yarmouth Central Library, Great Yarmouth
http://www.norfolk.gov.uk/council/departments/lis/nsyar.htm

✳ King's Lynn Central Library, King's Lynn
http://www.norfolk.gov.uk/council/departments/lis/nslynn.htm

✳ Norfolk Studies Library, Norfolk and Norwich Central Library,
    Norwich
http://www.norfolk.gov.uk/council/departments/lis/nsref.htm

✳ Thetford Library
http://www.norfolk.gov.uk/council/departments/lis/nsthet.htm

INFORMATION SITES

Norfolk Record Office: Parish Registers Available on Microfiche
http://www.norfolk.gov.uk/council/departments/nro/nrofiche.htm

LISTS AND LINKS

* Norfolk GENUKI Home Page
http://www.uea.ac.uk/~s090/genuki/NFK/

❧ NORTHAMPTONSHIRE

Northamptonshire Record Office, Northampton
http://www.nro.northamptonshire.gov.uk/

Northamptonshire Central Library, Northampton
http://www.earl.org.uk/familia/services/northamptonshire.html

INFORMATION SITES

Northamptonshire Heritage
http://web.ukonline.co.uk/glenn.foard/webdoc9.htm

SELECTED DOCUMENTS AND INDEXES ONLINE

Map of Northampton, 1807
http://www.library.yale.edu/MapColl/nham807.htm

LISTS AND LINKS

* Northamptonshire GENUKI Home Page
http://www.skynet.co.uk/genuki/big/eng/NTH/

❧ NORTHUMBERLAND (see also Durham)

Northumberland Record Office, North Gosforth, Newcastle-upon-Tyne
http://www.swinhope.demon.co.uk/genuki/NBL/NorthumberlandRO/
    There are also branch offices in Morpeth and Berwick-upon-Tweed.

Newcastle Heritage Information Centre, Newcastle-upon-Tyne
http://www.newcastle.gov.uk/atoz.nsf/n/?openview

North Shields Central Library, North Tyneside
http://www.earl.org.uk/familia/services/north_tyneside.html

INFORMATION SITES

Berwick-upon-Tweed History
http://ourworld.compuserve.com/homepages/north_east_england_
    history_page/Berwicko.htm
    Berwick-upon-Tweed has changed hands between England and Scotland
    thirteen times.

County Northumberland History
http://ourworld.compuserve.com/homepages/north_east_england_
    history_page/NORTHUMBERLAND.htm

Mediaeval Northumberland
http://users.aol.com/muaddib721/medieval.htm

Northumberland Map and Gazetteer
http://www.northumberland.gov.uk/vg/gazeteer.html

Northumbria: The Ancient Kingdom of Northumberland
http://dspace.dial.pipex.com/town/square/ae565/ndtop.htm

Surnames of North Eastern England
http://ourworld.compuserve.com/homepages/north_east_england_
    history_page/SURNAMES.htm

SELECTED DOCUMENTS AND INDEXES ONLINE

Index of Place Names in Northumberland
http://www.swinhope.demon.co.uk/genuki/NBL/Gazetteer/

LISTS AND LINKS

✳ Northumberland GENUKI Home Page
http://www.swinhope.demon.co.uk/genuki/NBL/

✳ Northumberland Libraries with Family History Resources
http://www.earl.org.uk/familia/services/northumberland.html

❧ NOTTINGHAMSHIRE

Nottinghamshire Archives (Record Office), Nottingham
http://www.nottscc.gov.uk/libraries/Archives/welcome.htm

Nottingham Local Studies Library, Nottingham
http://www.earl.org.uk/familia/services/nottingham.html

INFORMATION SITES

Using Nottinghamshire Archives for Family History Research
http://www.nottscc.gov.uk/libraries/Archives/famhist/index.htm

LISTS AND LINKS

Listing of Churches in Nottinghamshire, All Denominations
http://www.john316.com/SOUTHWEL/CHURCHES/CHURCHIX.HTM

∗ Nottinghamshire GENUKI Home Page
http://www.homeusers.prestel.co.uk/renfrew/genuki/NTT

❧ OXFORDSHIRE

Centre for Oxfordshire Studies, Central Library, Westgate
http://www.earl.org.uk/familia/services/oxfords.html

Rhodes House Library, Oxford
http://www.bodley.ox.ac.uk/boris/guides/rhl/rhl01.html

INFORMATION SITES

∗ Oxfordshire County Museums Service Home Page
http://dspace.dial.pipex.com/town/drive/lt28/

SELECTED DOCUMENTS AND INDEXES ONLINE

Maps of Oxford, 1605, 1810, 1878, and 1921
http://www.rsl.ox.ac.uk/nnj/webmapsf.htm

LISTS AND LINKS

∗ Oxford GENUKI Home Page
http://users.ox.ac.uk/~malcolm/genuki/big/eng/OXF/

❧ RUTLAND (see also Leicestershire)

Rutland Record Office, Oakham
No Internet presence

Leicester and Rutland FHS, Wigston (Leicestershire)
http://www.geocities.com/Heartland/Pointe/3446/index.html

LISTS AND LINKS

✳ Rutland GENUKI Home Page
http://www.skynet.co.uk/genuki/big/eng/RUT/

✳ Rutland GenWeb Towns and Parishes
http://www.rootsweb.com/~engrut/townsandparishes.htm

❧ SHROPSHIRE (SALOP)

Shropshire Records and Research Centre, Shrewsbury
**http://www.shropshire-cc.gov.uk/80256640003d4431/
5fc64ff6df8336828025664800344e02/
6f682a43ac1654d38025667f003b2415?OpenDocument**
or
http://www.earl.org.uk/familia/services/shropshire.html

SELECTED DOCUMENTS AND INDEXES ONLINE

Map of Shropshire, ca. 1830
http://www.rsl.ox.ac.uk/nnj/webmapsf.htm

LISTS AND LINKS

✳ Shropshire GENUKI Home Page
http://www.essex.ac.uk/AMS/genuki/SAL/

❧ SOMERSET

Somerset Record Office, Taunton
http://www.somerset.gov.uk/archives/

Bath Central Library, Bath
http://www.earl.org.uk/familia/services/bath_ne_somerset.html

Somerset Studies Library, Taunton
http://www.earl.org.uk/familia/services/somerset.html

Weston Library, Weston-Super-Mare
http://www.earl.org.uk/familia/services/north_somerset.html

SELECTED DOCUMENTS AND INDEXES ONLINE

Map of the City of Bath, 1676
http://www.library.yale.edu/MapColl/bathe.htm

INFORMATION SITES

A Guide to Tracing Your Family History in the Somerset Record Office
http://www.somerset.gov.uk/archives/yosomfam.htm

LISTS AND LINKS

* Somerset GENUKI Home Page
http://www.genuki.org.uk/big/eng/SOM/

❧ STAFFORDSHIRE

Smethwick Library, Community History and Archives Service,
    Smethwick
http://www.earl.org.uk/familia/services/sandwell.html

Walsall Local History Centre, Walsall
http://www.earl.org.uk/familia/services/walsall.html

Wolverhampton Archives and Local Studies Library, Wolverhampton
http://www.earl.org.uk/familia/services/wolverhampton.html

INFORMATION SITES

* Black Country Pages
http://www.geocities.com/Heartland/Prairie/6697
> Serves "The Black Country" in the West Midlands region of Worcester
> and Staffordshire: Brierley Hill, Dudley (which was an "island" of
> Worcestershire within Staffordshire), Halesowen, Lye, Stourbridge,
> Walsall, Wednesbury, West Bromwich, and Wolverhampton.

History of Victorian Wolverhampton
http://www.scit.wlv.ac.uk/~cm1906/victorian.wton.html

SELECTED DOCUMENTS AND INDEXES ONLINE

Pigot's and Slater's Topography of the British Isles: Staffordshire and the
 Potteries
http://www.staffs.ac.uk/schools/humanities_and_soc_sciences/census/
 pigstart.htm

LISTS AND LINKS

❉ Staffordshire GENUKI Home Page
http://www.genuki.org.uk/big/eng/STS/

❉ Staffordshire Libraries with Family History Resources
http://www.earl.org.uk/familia/services/staffordshire.html

❧ SUFFOLK

Suffolk Record Office, Central Library, Lowestoft
http://www.suffolkcc.gov.uk/libraries_and_heritage/sro/index.html

Suffolk FHS
http://www.genuki.org.uk/big/eng/SFK/sfhs/sfhs.htm

INFORMATION SITES

History of Haverhill
http://www.langley.co.uk/haverhill/history.htm

SELECTED DOCUMENTS AND INDEXES ONLINE

Suffolk Surname List
http://www.visualcreations.com/pers/leeann/suffolk/

LISTS AND LINKS

❉ Suffolk GENUKI Home Page
http://www.genuki.org.uk/big/eng/SFK/

❋ Suffolk Libraries with Family History Resources
http://www.earl.org.uk/familia/services/suffolk.html

✌ SURREY

Surrey History Service, Woking
http://shs.surreycc.gov.uk/
> The History Service was formed by the merger of the former Surrey Record Office, based in County Hall in Kingston, the Guildford Muniment Room, and the Surrey Local Studies Library.

(London Borough of) Sutton Archive and Local Studies Search Room, Sutton
http://www.earl.org.uk/partners/sutton/archive.html
> The Local Studies Collection relates particularly to this Borough and more generally to Surrey and Greater London (especially south of the Thames). The Borough's Archives are kept separately from the Local Studies Collection, with the exception of Wallington (previously Croydon) Magistrates Court and copies of Surrey parish registers.

SELECTED DOCUMENTS AND INDEXES ONLINE

Surrey Archives Index Database
http://shs.surreycc.gov.uk/

LISTS AND LINKS

❋ Surrey GENUKI Home Page
http://www.gold.ac.uk/genuki/SRY/

✌ SUSSEX

East Sussex County Record Office, Lewes
http://www.eastsussexcc.gov.uk/council/services/general/archives/main.htm

West Sussex Records Office, Chichester
http://www.westsussex.gov.uk/cs/ro/rohome.htm

Brighton Reference Library, Brighton
http://www.earl.org.uk/familia/services/brighton_hove.html

Worthing Library, Worthing
http://www.earl.org.uk/familia/services/west_sussex.html

INFORMATION SITES

West Sussex Special Collections
http://www.westsussex.gov.uk/li/wsussex.htm

LISTS AND LINKS

✻ Public Libraries in East Sussex
http://www.eastsussexcc.gov.uk/council/services/lib/cntylib/main.htm

✻ Sussex GENUKI Home Page
http://www.gold.ac.uk/genuki/SSX/

✻ West Sussex Parish Councils Index
http://www.westsussex.gov.uk/cs/parish/parishindex.htm

❧ WARWICKSHIRE

Warwickshire County Record Office, Warwick
http://www.warwickshire.gov.uk/general/rcindex.htm
> The archive material covers the historic county of Warwickshire, but for most purposes excludes Birmingham, Coventry, and Stratford-on-Avon where there are separate record offices.

Birmingham Central Library, Local Studies and History Service, Birmingham
http://www.earl.org.uk/familia/services/birmingham.html

Coventry Central Library, Local Studies, Coventry
http://www.earl.org.uk/familia/services/coventry.html

Coventry FHS, Coventry
http://www.coventry.org.uk/heritage/familyhistory/index.html

Solihull Central Library, Information and Local Studies Section, Solihull
http://www.earl.org.uk/familia/services/solihull.html

Spon End and Lower Coundon History Group, Coventry
http://www.geocities.com/CollegePark/3384/

University of Warwick Library, Modern Records Centre, Warwick
http://www.warwick.ac.uk/services/library/mrc/mrc.html
Material held includes trade union registry files and records of employers and trade associations.

Warwick Library, Warwick
http://www.earl.org.uk/familia/services/warwickshire.html

INFORMATION SITES

Tracing Your Ancestors in Warwickshire
http://www.warwickshire.gov.uk/general/ancestor.htm

LISTS AND LINKS

* Warwickshire GENUKI Home Page
http://www.genuki.org.uk/big/eng/WAR/

❧ WESTMORLAND (see also Cumberland)

The counties of Cumberland and Westmorland, the Furness District of Lancashire (Lonsdale north of the Sands), and the parishes of Dent, Garsdale, and Sedbergh in the former West Riding of Yorkshire were formed into the administrative county of Cumbria in 1974. Records from these areas can be found in the offices of the Cumbria Archive Service at Barrow-in-Furness, Carlisle, Kendal, and Whitehaven. Records relating to the north and east of the historic county of Cumberland are in the Carlisle office. The Record Office and Local Studies Library in Whitehaven houses records relating to places south and west of the River Derwent and north of the River Duddon. Records relating to the former county of Westmorland and the Sedbergh district are in Kendal. Those records relating to Furness are in the Barrow office.

LISTS AND LINKS

* Westmorland GENUKI Home Page
http://www.awitc.demon.co.uk/genuki/WES/

❧ WILTSHIRE

Wiltshire Record Office, Trowbridge
No Internet presence

LISTS AND LINKS

* Wiltshire GENUKI Home Page
http://www.genuki.org.uk/big/eng/WIL/

* Wiltshire Libraries with Family History Resources
http://www.earl.org.uk/familia/services/wiltshire.html

❧ WORCESTERSHIRE

In 1974 the former counties of Herefordshire and Worcestershire were combined to form Hereford and Worcester. It was then divided into nine districts: Bromsgrove, Leominster, Malvern Hills, Redditch, South Herefordshire, Wychavon, Wyre Forest, and the cities of Hereford and Worcester. In 1998 a new unitary authority for Herefordshire and a county council for Worcestershire replaced the administrative county of Hereford and Worcester.

Worcestershire Record Office, County Hall, Worcester
http://www.worcestershire.gov.uk/wcc/dir_corp/records/homepage.htm

Dudley Archives and Local History Service, Coseley
http://dudley.gov.uk/about/history/further/archives.htm

INFORMATION SITES

* Black Country Pages
http://www.geocities.com/Heartland/Prairie/6697
Serves "The Black Country" in the West Midlands region of Worcester and Staffordshire: Brierley Hill, Dudley (which was an "island" of Worcestershire within Staffordshire), Halesowen, Lye, Stourbridge, Walsall, Wednesbury, West Bromwich, and Wolverhampton.

Genealogical Resources in Worcestershire
http://193.128.154.20/pages/h&w_cc/wor_rec1.htm

The History of Kempsey
http://www.geocities.com/Athens/Academy/5386

SELECTED DOCUMENTS AND INDEXES ONLINE

Map of Worcester, 1808
http://www.library.yale.edu/MapColl/worc1808.htm

LISTS AND LINKS

✳ Worcestershire GENUKI Home Page
http://www.genuki.org.uk/big/eng/WOR/

✳ Worcestershire Libraries with Family History Resources
http://www.earl.org.uk/familia/services/worcester.html

❧ YORKSHIRE

West Yorkshire Archive Service (Bradford, Calderdale, Kirklees, Leeds, and Wakefield)
http://www.archives.wyjs.org.uk

Barnsley Central Library, Barnsley
http://www.earl.org.uk/familia/services/barnsley.html

Calderdale Central Library, Halifax
http://www.earl.org.uk/familia/services/calderdale.html

Doncaster Central Library, Local History Library, Waterdale, Doncaster
http://www.earl.org.uk/familia/services/doncaster.html

Kingston-upon-Hull Central Library, Local Studies Library, Hull
http://www.open.gov.uk/hullcc/libraries/history/famhist1.htm
Genealogical material for Hull, the East Riding, and northern Lincolnshire.

Leeds Local and Family History Library, Leeds
http://www.leeds.gov.uk/library/services/locnfam.html

Middlesbrough Central Reference Library, Middlesbrough
http://www.middlesbrough.gov.uk/mcrl.htm

Rotherham Central Library Archives and Local Studies Section, Rotherham
http://www.rotherham.gov.uk/

Sheffield Central Library, Sheffield
http://www.earl.org.uk/partners/sheffield/index.html

Sheffield Archives Service
http://www.earl.org.uk/partners/sheffield/arch.htm

University of Huddersfield, Archives and Special Collections, Huddersfield
http://www.hud.ac.uk/schools/library/libarch.htm

University of Hull, Brynmor Jones Library, Archives and Special Collections, Hull
http://www.hull.ac.uk/lib/archives/

University of York, Borthwick Institute of Historical Research, York
http://www.york.ac.uk/inst/bihr/

Wakefield Central Library, Wakefield
http://www.earl.org.uk/familia/services/wakefield.html

Whitby Archives and Heritage Center, Whitby
http://www.users.zetnet.co.uk/whitby-archives/

York Central Library, Reference and Information Service, York
http://www.earl.org.uk/familia/services/york.html

INFORMATION SITES

History of Richmond (North Yorkshire Dales)
http://dspace.dial.pipex.com/town/parade/hq69/

Yorkshire History
http://ourworld.compuserve.com/homepages/north_east_england_
history_page/Yorkshire_Page.htm

SELECTED DOCUMENTS AND INDEXES ONLINE

Asda's Yorkshire/English Phrase Book
http://www.yorkshirenet.co.uk/yorkshireday/ydphrase.html

Emigrants of Yorkshire: Emigration from Yorkshire and Durham in the Eighteenth Century (database)
http://www.karoo.net/eminorame/

Hull's Fishing Heritage in Photographs
http://dspace.dial.pipex.com/town/street/tp90/

Topographical Dictionary of Yorkshire for the Year 1822, by Thomas Langdale
http://www.genuki.org.uk/big/eng/YKS/yrksdict/

LISTS AND LINKS

❋ East Riding of Yorkshire Libraries with Family History Resources
http://www.earl.org.uk/familia/services/east_riding.html

❋ North Yorkshire Libraries with Family History Resources
http://www.earl.org.uk/familia/services/north_yorks.html

❋ Yorkshire GENUKI Home Page
http://www.blunham.demon.co.uk/genuki/YKS/

THE CHURCH OF ENGLAND

The Church of England is organized in England, the Isle of Man, the Channel Islands, the Isles of Scilly, and a small part of Wales. Diocesan boundaries have never followed political or administrative boundaries. The current dioceses for the Church of England are listed with areas of service—now or in the past—given in parentheses, if they include significantly more than the place name indicated by the title of the diocese. For the Anglican Church in Wales, see under Wales. Parish registers are usually deposited with local civil authorities; however, many diocesan sites have maps and addresses for individual parishes and deaneries.

Church of England Home Page
http://www.church-of-england.org/

❋ Links to Dioceses of the Church of England
http://www.church-of-england.org/location/location.html

❋ Diocese of Bath and Wells Parish Links (Somerset and Wiltshire)
http://www.bathwells.anglican.org/parindex.htm

Diocese of Birmingham (Warwickshire)
No Internet presence

❋ Diocese of Blackburn Parish Links (Lancashire)
http://web.ukonline.co.uk/anchorsholme/diodir/websites.htm

❋ Diocese of Bradford Parish Links (Bradford and Keighley, Cumbria, Lancashire, and North Yorkshire)
http://www.bradford.anglican.org/online.htm

Diocese of Bristol (Gloucestershire)
No Internet presence

Diocese of Canterbury (Kent and parts of Essex and Sussex)
No Internet presence

Diocese of Carlisle (Cumberland)
No Internet presence

Diocese of Chelmsford (Essex)
No Internet presence

Diocese of Chester (Cheshire and parts of Flintshire)
No Internet presence

Diocese of Chichester (Sussex and parts of Essex)
No Internet presence

Diocese of Coventry (Warwickshire)
No Internet presence

Diocese of Derby (Derbyshire)
No Internet presence

✳ Diocese of Durham Parish Links (Durham and parts of Yorkshire)
http://www.durham.anglican.org/

✳ Diocese of Ely Parish Links (Cambridgeshire and parts of
    Bedfordshire, Buckinghamshire, Huntingdonshire, Norfolk, and
    Sussex)
http://www.ely.anglican.org/gazette.html

Diocese of Exeter (Devon and parts of Cornwall)
No Internet presence

Diocese of Gloucester (Gloucestershire)
http://www.doma.demon.co.uk/glosdioc.htm

Diocese of Guildford (Surrey)
No Internet presence

Diocese of Hereford (Herefordshire and parts of Gloucestershire,
    Montgomeryshire, Radnorshire, Shropshire, and Worcestershire)
No Internet presence

✳ Diocese of Leicester Parish Links (Leicestershire and parts of
    Nottinghamshire)
http://homepages.webleicester.co.uk/mcourt/parish.htm

✳ Diocese of Lichfield Parish Links (Staffordshire and parts of
    Derbyshire, Lancashire, Shropshire, and Warwickshire)
http://www.broadnet.co.uk/community/church/anglican/lichfield/
    parish.htm

Diocese of Lincoln (Lincolnshire)
No Internet presence

Diocese of Liverpool (Lancashire)
No Internet presence

Diocese of London (London and parts of Essex, Hertfordshire, and
    Middlesex)
No Internet presence

Diocese of Manchester (Lancashire)
No Internet presence

Diocese of Newcastle (Northumberland)
No Internet presence

Diocese of Norwich (Norfolk)
No Internet presence

✳ Diocese of Oxford Parish Links (Berkshire, Buckinghamshire, and
    Oxfordshire)
http://www.oxford.anglican.org/Parishes/

✳ Diocese of Peterborough Parish and Deanery Links
    (Northamptonshire and Rutland)
http://www.peterborough-diocese.org.uk/

Diocese of Portsmouth (Hampshire)
No Internet presence

✳ Diocese of Ripon Parish Links (Yorkshire)
http://ourworld.compuserve.com/homepages/riponcc/parish.htm

✳ Diocese of Rochester Parish Links (Kent and parts of
    Buckinghamshire and Hertfordshire)
http://www.anglican.org.uk/rochester/

✷ Diocese of St. Albans Parish and Deanery Links (Hertfordshire and
parts of Bedfordshire, Buckinghamshire, and North London)
http://www.stalbansdioc.org.uk/

Diocese of St. Edmundsbury and Ipswich (Suffolk)
No Internet presence

✷ Diocese of Salisbury Parish and Deanery Links (Wiltshire)
http://www.eluk.co.uk/spireweb/deanery.html

Diocese of Sheffield (Yorkshire)
**http://web.ukonline.co.uk/members/trafic/Diocese/
diocese%20index.htm**

Diocese of Sodor and Man (Isle of Man)
No Internet presence

✷ Diocese of Southwark Parish Links (South London, East Surrey)
http://www.roehampton.ac.uk/link/dswark/links.htm

Diocese of Southwell (Nottinghamshire)
http://www.john316.com/SOUTHWEL/SOUTHWEL.HTM

Diocese of Truro (Cornwall)
No Internet presence

✷ Diocese of Wakefield Deanery Links (Yorkshire)
http://www.anglican.org.uk/wakefield/parish.htm

✷ Diocese of Winchester Parish Links (Hampshire, the Channel Islands,
and East Dorset)
http://win.diocese.org.uk/parish.html

Diocese of Worcester (Worcestershire and parts of Gloucestershire,
Staffordshire, and Warwickshire)
No Internet presence

Diocese of York (Yorkshire)
No Internet presence

WALES

National Library of Wales/Llyfrgell Genedlaethol Cymru
http://www.llgc.org.uk/lc/lcs0001.htm

Museum of Welsh Life, St. Fagans, Cardiff
http://www.cardiff.ac.uk/nmgw/mwl/mwlcoll.html

University of Wales Bangor, Main Library, Department of Manuscripts,
    Bangor
http://www.llgc.org.uk/cac/cac0024.htm
    Collections include everything relating to North Wales, but especially estate
    papers, papers relating to Welsh language and literature, the papers of
    Non-conformist causes, and industrial and maritime papers.

University of Wales Swansea, Local Archive Collections, Swansea
http://www.swan.ac.uk/lis/archives/

INFORMATION SITES

✳ Early Emigration from Wales
http://www.data-wales.co.uk/emig1.htm

Emigration from Wales to America
http://www.data-wales.co.uk/emmap.htm

A Guide to Genealogical Sources at National Library of Wales
http://www.llgc.org.uk/lc/gg01.htm

Guided Tour: The Principality of Wales
http://www.cs.brown.edu/fun/welsh/home.html

Museum of Welsh Life Manuscripts Collection
http://www.cardiff.ac.uk/nmgw/mwl/mwlarch.html

Quaker Records in Wales
http://www.qfhs.mcmail.com/counties/wales.htm

Welsh Patronymics
http://www.users.globalnet.co.uk/~wyside01/helps/patronym.htm

SELECTED DOCUMENTS AND INDEXES ONLINE

The Data Wales Maps Page
http://www.data-wales.co.uk/walesmap.htm

LISTS AND LINKS

✳ Wales GENUKI Home Page
http://www.genuki.org.uk/big/wal/

✳ Wales GenWeb Project
http://www.rootsweb.com/~engwales/

✳ Welsh Archives Council: Archive Repositories
http://www.llgc.org.uk/cac/cac0050.htm

❧ ANGLESEY

From 1974 to 1996 Anglesey was part of the county of Gwynedd.

✳ Isle of Anglesey County Council/Cyngor Sir Ynys Môn, Llangefni
http://www.anglesey.gov.uk/english/library/index.htm

Gwynedd FHS/Cymdeithas Hanes Teuluoedd Gwynedd
http://www.nol.co.uk/~gwyfhs/

INFORMATION SITES

✳ Anglesey History Site
http://www.kovcomp.co.uk/anglesey.html

LISTS AND LINKS

✳ Anglesey GENUKI Home Page
http://www.genuki.org.uk/big/wal/AGY/

❧ BRECONSHIRE (BRECKNOCKSHIRE)
(see also Radnorshire)

The counties of Breconshire, Montgomeryshire, and Radnorshire became the county of Powys in 1974.

Powys County Archives Office, Llandrindod Wells
http://www.powys.gov.uk/english/education/archives/
> Established in 1991 to serve Powys County Council, incorporating the former counties (and District Councils) of Breconshire, Montgomeryshire, and Radnorshire.

Brecon Area Library, Brecon
http://www.earl.org.uk/familia/services/powys.html

Powys FHS/Cymdeithas Hanes Teuluoedd Powys
http://ourworld.compuserve.com/homepages/michaelmacsorley/
>> powys1.htm
> Serves the former historic counties of Breconshire, Montgomeryshire, and Radnorshire, which now form the county of Powys.

INFORMATION SITES

✳ Introduction to Powys Towns
http://www.powys.gov.uk/english/home/powys/towns/
> Builth Wells, Brecon, Crickhowell, Hay-on-Wye, Knighton, Llandrindod Wells, Llanfair Caereinion, Llanfyllin, Llanidloes, Llanwrtyd Wells, Machynlleth, Montgomery, Newtown, Presteigne, Rhayader, Talgarth, Welshpool, and Ystradgynlais.

Powys Archives Guide to Holdings: Breconshire Records
http://www.powys.gov.uk/english/education/archives/info/brec/
>> BREC1.HTM

LISTS AND LINKS

✳ Breconshire GENUKI Home Page
http://www.rapidagent.co.uk/genuki/BRE/

❧ CAERNARFONSHIRE
(CAERNARVONSHIRE)

Caernarfonshire became part of the county of Gwynedd in 1974.

Caernarfon Record Office, Gwynedd Archives and Museums Service, Caernarfon
http://www.llgc.org.uk/cac/cac0053.htm

Conwy Archives Service, Llandudno Library, Llandudno
http://www.llgc.org.uk/cac/cac0035.htm
> Established in 1996 when the new unitary authority of Conwy County Borough Council was formed. It serves the county borough of Conwy and its predecessor authorities (the Aberconwy District of old Caernarfonshire and the Colwyn District of old Denbighshire).

Gwynedd FHS: See under Anglesey

Llyfrgell Caernarfon, Lon Pafiliwn, Caernarfon
http://www.earl.org.uk/familia/services/gwynedd.html

LISTS AND LINKS

✳ Caernarfonshire GENUKI Home Page
http://www.genuki.org.uk/big/wal/CAE/

⚘ CARDIGANSHIRE (CEREDIGION)

> Cardiganshire, Carmarthenshire, and Pembrokeshire became part of the administrative county of Dyfed in 1974. Cardiganshire was reinstated as a county under the name of Ceredigion in 1996.

Ceredigion County Archives Service, Aberystwyth
http://www.llgc.org.uk/cac/cac0009.htm

Aberystwyth Public Library, Aberystwyth
http://www.earl.org.uk/familia/services/ceredigion.html

Cardiganshire FHS/Cymdeithas Hanes Teuluoedd Ceredigion
http://www.celtic.co.uk/~heaton/cgnfhs/

Dyfed FHS/Cymdeithas Hanes Teuluoedd Dyfed
http://www.westwales.co.uk/dfhs/dfhs.htm
> Serves the counties of Carmarthenshire, Ceredigion (Cardiganshire), and Pembrokeshire.

SELECTED DOCUMENTS AND INDEXES ONLINE

Pigot's and Slater's Topography of the British Isles: Cardiff
http://www.staffs.ac.uk/schools/humanities_and_soc_sciences/census/
   pigstart.htm

LISTS AND LINKS

✳ Cardiganshire GENUKI Home Page
http://www.semlyn.demon.co.uk/genuki/CGN/

❧ CARMARTHENSHIRE

Cardiganshire, Carmarthenshire, and Pembrokeshire became part of the administrative county of Dyfed in 1974. Carmarthenshire was reestablished as a county in 1996.

Carmarthenshire County Archives Service, Carmarthen
http://www.llgc.org.uk/cac/cac0028.htm

Dyfed FHS: See under Cardiganshire

LISTS AND LINKS

✳ Carmarthenshire GENUKI Home Page
http://www.semlyn.demon.co.uk/genuki/CMN/

✳ Carmarthenshire Libraries with Family History Resources
http://www.earl.org.uk/familia/services/carmarthenshire.html

❧ DENBIGHSHIRE (see also Caernarfonshire)

The County of Clwyd was created in 1974 from the ancient counties of Flintshire, most of Denbighshire, and part of Merionethshire. The county of Clwyd ceased to exist and four new unitary authorities were created in 1996: Denbighshire, Flintshire, Conwy County Borough, and Wrexham County Borough.

Denbighshire Record Office, Ruthin
http://www.llgc.org.uk/cac/cac0011.htm

Wrexham Archives Service, Wrexham
http://www.llgc.org.uk/cac/cac0038.htm
Serves parts of the pre-1974 counties of Denbighshire and Flintshire and records of those counties are held at the Denbighshire Record Office at Ruthin and the Flintshire Record Office at Hawarden.

Clwyd FHS/Cymdeithas Hanes Teuluoedd Clwyd, Ruthin
http://www.genuki.org.uk/big/wal/DEN/CWDFHS/

Wrexham Library and Arts Centre, Wrexham
http://www.earl.org.uk/familia/services/wrexham.html

LISTS AND LINKS

* Denbighshire GENUKI Home Page
http://www.genuki.org.uk/big/wal/DEN/

❧ FLINTSHIRE

The County of Clwyd was created in 1974 from the ancient counties of Flintshire, most of Denbighshire, and part of Merionethshire. The county of Clwyd ceased to exist and four new unitary authorities were created in 1996: Denbighshire, Flintshire, Conwy County Borough, and Wrexham County Borough.

Flintshire Record Office, Hawarden
http://www.llgc.org.uk/cac/cac0032.htm

Clwyd FHS: See under Denbighshire

Flintshire Reference and Information Centre, Mold
http://www.earl.org.uk/familia/services/flintshire.html

LISTS AND LINKS

* Flintshire GENUKI Home Page
http://www.genuki.org.uk/big/wal/FLN/

❧ GLAMORGANSHIRE

In 1974 Glamorgan was divided into the counties of Mid Glamorgan, South Glamorgan, and West Glamorgan. In 1996 Mid Glamorgan and South Glamorgan reunited as Glamorgan, with West Glamorgan remaining a separate county.

Glamorgan Record Office, Cardiff
http://www.llgc.org.uk/cac/cac0026.htm
> Holds historic records relating to the geographic area of the former Mid Glamorgan and South Glamorgan County Councils, and ecclesiastical parish records of the Diocese of Llandaff.

West Glamorgan County Archive Service, Swansea
http://www.llgc.org.uk/cac/cac0019.htm
> Established in 1982 as a branch of the Glamorgan Record Office. It became an independent County Archive Service in 1992. Local authorities served: the city and county of Swansea, and Neath Port Talbot County Borough.

Bridgend Reference and Information Centre and Local Studies Library, Bridgend
http://www.earl.org.uk/familia/services/bridgend.html

Cardiff Central Library, Local Studies Department, Cardiff
http://www.earl.org.uk/familia/services/cardiff_county.html

Caerphilly County Local Studies Centre, Bargoed
http://www.caerphilly.gov.uk/libraries.html

Glamorgan FHS/Gymdeithas Hanes Teuluoedd Morgannwg
http://members.aol.com/gfhsoc/

Merthyr Tydfil Central Library, Merthyr Tydfil
http://www.earl.org.uk/familia/services/merthyr.html

Neath Library, County Archives Service, Neath
http://www.earl.org.uk/familia/services/vale_of_glamorgan.html

Neath Reference Library, Neath
http://www.earl.org.uk/familia/services/neath_neath.html

Port Talbot Reference Library, Port Talbot
http://www.earl.org.uk/familia/services/neath_port_talbot.html

Swansea Central Reference Library, Swansea
http://www.earl.org.uk/familia/services/swansea.html

LISTS AND LINKS

* Glamorgan GENUKI Home Page
http://www.genuki.org.uk/big/wal/GLA/

❧ MERIONETHSHIRE (see also Denbighshire)

In 1974 part of Merionethshire became the county of Clwyd and most of it became part of the county of Gwynedd. The county of Clwyd ceased to exist and four new unitary authorities were created in 1996: Denbighshire, Flintshire, Conwy County Borough, and Wrexham County Borough. The Denbighshire Record Office in Ruthin holds some post-1974 records for the Edeirnion District of Merioneth.

Merioneth Record Office, Dolgellau
http://www.llgc.org.uk/cac/cac0030.htm

Gwynedd FHS: See under Anglesey

LISTS AND LINKS

✳ Merionethshire GENUKI Home Page
http://www.genuki.org.uk/big/wal/MER

❧ MONMOUTHSHIRE

The ancient county of Monmouthshire has sometimes been considered an English county because of court jurisdictions dating from the sixteenth century. In 1974 it became the county of Gwent. In 1996 Monmouth Borough Council and Gwent County Council were abolished and Monmouthshire County Council was created, covering only the eastern half of what was once the old historic county. Administrative functions were assumed by the new unitary authorities of Blaenau Gwent, Caerphilly, Monmouthshire, Newport, and Torfaen.

Gwent Record Office, Cwmbrân
http://www.llgc.org.uk/cac/cac0004.htm
Established in 1938 as the Monmouthshire Record Office. It has served Monmouthshire County Council (1938–1974), Gwent County Council (1974–1996), and Blaenau Gwent County Borough Council, Caerphilly County Borough Council, Monmouthshire County Council, Newport County Borough Council, and Torfaen County Borough Council (1996–present).

Ebbw Vale Library, Ebbw Vale
http://www.earl.org.uk/familia/services/blaenau_gwent.html

Gwent FHS, Pontypool
http://www.riggs.ndirect.co.uk/GwentFHS/Index.htm

Newport Central Reference Library, Newport
http://www.earl.org.uk/partners/newport/familyhist.html

INFORMATION SITES

Monmouthshire County Council Directory of Local Organisations
http://www.earl.org.uk/partners/monmouthshire/voldirect.html

Monmouthshire Libraries and Information Services, Cwmbrân
http://www.earl.org.uk/partners/monmouthshire/

LISTS AND LINKS

✽ Monmouthshire GENUKI Home Page
http://www.genuki.org.uk/big/wal/MON/index.html#index

⊱ MONTGOMERYSHIRE
(see also Radnorshire)

The counties of Breconshire, Montgomeryshire, and Radnorshire became
the County of Powys in 1974.

Powys County Archives Office, Llandrindod Wells
http://www.powys.gov.uk/english/education/archives/
Established in 1991 to serve Powys County Council, incorporating the
former counties (and District Councils) of Breconshire, Montgomeryshire,
and Radnorshire.

Powys FHS: See under Breconshire

INFORMATION SITES

Crime and Punishment in Montgomeryshire
http://www.powys.gov.uk/english/education/archives/Newtown/
    first.HTM

✽ Introduction to Powys Towns
http://www.powys.gov.uk/english/home/powys/towns/
    Builth Wells, Brecon, Crickhowell, Hay-on-Wye, Knighton, Llandrindod
    Wells, Llanfair Caereinion, Llanfyllin, Llanidloes, Llanwrtyd Wells,
    Machynlleth, Montgomery, Newtown, Presteigne, Rhayader, Talgarth,
    Welshpool, and Ystradgynlais.

Powys Archives Guide to Holdings: Montgomeryshire Records
http://www.powys.gov.uk/english/education/archives/info/mont/MONT1.HTM

LISTS AND LINKS

⁜ Montgomeryshire GENUKI Home Page
http://www.rapidagent.co.uk/genuki/MGY/

❧ PEMBROKESHIRE

Cardiganshire, Carmathenshire, and Pembrokeshire became part of the administrative county of Dyfed in 1974. Pembrokeshire was reinstated as a county in 1996.

Pembrokeshire Record Office, Haverfordwest
http://www.llgc.org.uk/cac/cac0002.htm

Dyfed FHS: See under Cardiganshire

Pembrokeshire County Library, Haverfordwest
http://www.earl.org.uk/familia/services/pembrokes.html

LISTS AND LINKS

⁜ Pembrokeshire GENUKI Home Page
http://www.semlyn.demon.co.uk/genuki/PEM/

❧ RADNORSHIRE

The counties of Breconshire, Montgomeryshire, and Radnorshire became the County of Powys in 1974.

Powys County Archives Office, Llandrindod Wells
http://www.powys.gov.uk/english/education/archives/
Established in 1991 to serve Powys County Council, incorporating the former counties (and District Councils) of Breconshire, Montgomeryshire, and Radnorshire.

Powys FHS: See under Breconshire

INFORMATION SITES

* Introduction to Powys Towns
http://www.powys.gov.uk/english/home/powys/towns/
> Builth Wells, Brecon, Crickhowell, Hay-on-Wye, Knighton, Llandrindod Wells, Llanfair Caereinion, Llanfyllin, Llanidloes, Llanwrtyd Wells, Machynlleth, Montgomery, Newtown, Presteigne, Rhayader, Talgarth, Welshpool, and Ystradgynlais.

Powys Archives Guide to Holdings: Radnorshire Records
http://www.powys.gov.uk/english/education/archives/info/rad/
> **RADN1.HTM**

Powys Digital History Project
http://history.powys.org.uk/

LISTS AND LINKS

* Radnorshire GENUKI Home Page
http://www.rapidagent.co.uk/genuki/RAD/

THE (ANGLICAN) CHURCH IN WALES

The (Anglican) Church in Wales
http://www.churchinwales.org.uk/

* Parish Links in the Dioceses of the Church in Wales
http://www.churchinwales.org.uk/Diocese.html

Diocese of Bangor (Cardiganshire)
http://web.ukonline.co.uk/Members/church.beddgelert/ediocese.htm

Diocese of Llandaff (Glamorganshire)
http://www.churchinwales.org.uk/Llandaff/indlc.html

Diocese of Monmouth (Monmouthshire)
http://www.churchinwales.org.uk/monmouth/index.html

Diocese of Swansea and Brecon (Breconshire and Glamorganshire)
http://members.aol.com/swanbrecon/Index.htm

SCOTLAND

General Register Office (GRO), Edinburgh
http://www.open.gov.uk/gros/groshome.htm
    Civil registration (births, deaths, and marriages), census enumerations, and Old Parochial Registers (Church of Scotland).

National Archives of Scotland (formerly the Scottish Record Office), Edinburgh
Site is under development. The domain name, which is already registered, will be **http://www.nas.gov.uk**

Historic Scotland Library, Edinburgh
http://146.176.15.249/ISC1680

National Library of Scotland
http://www.nls.uk/

Scots Ancestry Research Society, Edinburgh
http://www.linnet.co.uk/linnet/tour/67010.htm

Scots Language Resource Centre, A.K. Bell Library, Perth
http://www.pkc.gov.uk/slrc/index.htm

Scottish Catholic Archives Library
http://146.176.15.249/ISC1763

✳ The Scottish Genealogy Society/Ceud Mile Failte, Edinburgh
http://www.sol.co.uk/s/scotgensoc/

Scottish Library, Edinburgh City Central Library, Edinburgh
http://146.176.15.249/ISC416

Scottish Military Historical Society, Glenboig, Lanarkshire
http://subnet.virtual-pc.com/~mc546367/journal.htm

University of Edinburgh, School of Scottish Studies, Edinburgh
http://www.pearl.arts.ed.ac.uk/SoSS/

INFORMATION SITES

Catalogue of All Newspapers, Books, Journals, and Manuscripts
    Preserved by the Scottish Newspapers Microfilming Unit
http://www.sol.co.uk/s/snmu/

Church of Scotland: History and Structure
http://www.cofs.org.uk/history.htmcolcos.htm
    The Church of Scotland is divided into twelve synods. Within the synods
    are a total of forty-nine presbyteries. The local church units are the con-
    gregations. Current synods are the synods of Argyll; Ayr; Clydesdale;
    Dumfries and Galloway; Fife; Forth; Grampian; Lothian; Perth and Angus;
    Ross, Sutherland, and Caithness; The Scottish Borders; and the South-
    ern Highlands.

✳ Church of Scotland Presbyteries
http://www.cofs.org.uk/presbyli.htm

✳ Church of Scotland Web Pages for Congregations
http://www.cofs.org.uk/congsite.htmlcos.htm

The Free Church of Scotland, Calvinist, Presbyterian, Covenanters,
    and Reformed
http://www.freechurch.org/

Genealogical Resources at Scottish Universities
http://www.ozemail.com.au/~jimjar/jimjargg.htm

A Guide to Family History by the Scottish Record Office (now known as
    the National Archives of Scotland)
http://www-saw.arts.ed.ac.uk/misc/genealogy/guide.html
    Holdings include wills, testaments, Services of Heirs (land inheritance),
    and estate records; Non-conformist church records and Kirk Session
    records; court and criminal records; Sasine (land-related) records, deeds,
    valuations (of property), and tax lists; and burgh records.

Impressions: Scottish Clan and Family Name Information
http://www.impressions.uk.com/

Introduction to Scottish Family History
http://www-theory.dcs.st-and.ac.uk/~mnd/genuki/intro.html

List of the Highland Clans
http://www.dalriada.co.uk/archives/clanlist.htm

List of Scottish Clan Septs and Dependents
http://www.electricscotland.com/webclans/septs.htm

Orthodox Churches in Scotland
http://www.geocities.com/Athens/Delphi/9438/index.html

✳ Scotland's Past
http://www.scotlandspast.com/

The Scots at War Project
http://www-saw.arts.ed.ac.uk/

The Scots Language: The Moray Claik
http://www.moray.org/scotsculture/

Scottish Civil Wars, 1638–1746
http://www.scotwar.ndirect.co.uk/

Scottish Clans and Families
http://www.electricscotland.com/webclans/index.html

Scottish Clan Web Board
http://www.electricscotland.com/theclans.htm

SELECTED DOCUMENTS AND INDEXES ONLINE

Gazetteer for Scotland Online
http://www.geo.ed.ac.uk/scotgaz/

Immigrant Ships Transcribers Guild: Scottish Ports
http://istg.rootsweb.com/departures/scotland.html
    Ports of Dundee, Glasgow, Greenock, and Lerwick.

Map of the Scottish Unitary Authorities
http://146.176.15.249/ISC3051

Scots Origins Database
http://www.origins.net/GRO/
    Scots Origins is an online fee-based database of fully searchable indexes
    of the GRO index to births/baptisms and banns/marriages from the Old
    Parish Registers dating from 1553 to 1854, plus the indexes to births,
    deaths, and marriages from 1855 to 1897.

The Scottish Office, Local Government Fact Sheet: New Local Authorities
(includes map)
http://www.scotland.gov.uk/library/documents3/fs12-11.htm

SCRAN (Scottish Cultural Resources Access Network)
http://www.scran.ac.uk/
  SCRAN is a fee-based, fully searchable resource base of Scottish material culture and human history. It works with museums, galleries, archives, and universities to digitize selected parts of their collections.

A Summary of Scottish Regiments in North America, 18th, 19th, and 20th
  Centuries, by Kim Stacy
http://www.virtual-pc.com/journal/naindex.htm

Tayside A Maritime History (TAMH) Searchable Databases
http://www.dmcsoft.com/tamh/index.php3?UID=36ad29bb3bdd5
  Contains four databases: Mariners and Voyages (shipping log records of
  mariners and voyages to and from Tayside ports), People (with links into
  historical records), Trading Ports Information, and Newspaper Articles.

LISTS AND LINKS

✳ Links to Scottish Academic Libraries
http://www.nls.uk/

✳ National Museums of Scotland
http://www.nms.ac.uk/

✳ Scotland GENUKI Home Page
http://www-theory.dcs.st-and.ac.uk/~mnd/genuki/scot.html

✳ Scotland GenWeb Project
http://www.rootsweb.com/~sctwgw/

✳ Scottish Links from Everything Celtic on the Web
http://celt.net/og/angscot.htm

✳ Scottish Military Museums
http://www.virtual-pc.com/journal/disp_018.htm

፝ ABERDEENSHIRE

In 1975 Aberdeenshire became part of the administrative region of Grampian. It was established as the county council of Aberdeenshire in 1996, with a separate city council for the City of Aberdeen.

Aberdeenshire County Council
http://www.aberdeenshire.gov.uk/
Serves parts of the old counties of Aberdeenshire, Banffshire, and Kincardineshire.

Aberdeen City Archives, Town House Branch
http://146.176.15.249/ISC1551

Aberdeen N.E. Scotland Family History Society
http://www.rsc.co.uk/anesfhs/
Serves the old counties of Aberdeenshire, Banffshire, Kincardineshire, and Morayshire.

Aberdeen University, Centre for Scottish Studies, Old Aberdeen
http://146.176.15.249/ISC1474

Aberdeenshire Local Studies Library, Oldmeldrum
http://www.aberdeenshire.gov.uk/famhist.htm

INFORMATION SITES

Aberdeenshire Museums
http://www.aberdeenshire.gov.uk/museums.htm

History of Aberdeen
http://www.regionlink.com/grampian/aberdeen/aberdeen.html

North East Newspapers Held by the North East of Scotland
Library Service
http://www.aberdeenshire.gov.uk/ne_news.htm

LISTS AND LINKS

✳ Aberdeenshire GENUKI Home Page
http://www.urie.demon.co.uk/genuki/ABD/aberdeen.htm

ANGUS (FORFAR)

In 1975 Angus became part of the administrative region of Tayside. It was established as the county council of Angus in 1996, with a separate city council for the City of Dundee.

Angus Archives, William Coull Anderson Library of Genealogy, Arbroath
http://www.angus.gov.uk/history/genealogy/default.htm

Dundee City Archive and Record Centre, Dundee
http://www.dundeecity.gov.uk/dcchtml/sservices/archives.html

Dundee University Archives, Dundee
http://www.dundee.ac.uk/archives/

Forfar and District Historical Society
http://www.dundee.ac.uk/~anicoll/FDHS/welcome.htm

Tay Valley FHS Research Center, Dundee
http://www.sol.co.uk/t/tayvalleyfhs/rescent/rescent.htm

LISTS AND LINKS

* Angus (Fofar) GENUKI Home Page
http://www.dundee.ac.uk/~anicoll/genuki/ANS/

ARGYLLSHIRE

In 1975 Argyllshire became part of the administrative regions of The Highlands and of Strathclyde. It was established as the county council of Argyll and Bute in 1996.

Argyll and Bute Local Studies Library, Library and Information Services, Dunoon
http://www.cqm.co.uk/ab_leisure/lib.html

Argyll and Bute Council Museum and Heritage Organisations
http://www.cqm.co.uk/ab_leisure/musher.html

LISTS AND LINKS

✳ Argyllshire GENUKI Home Page
http://www.roe.ac.uk/genuki/argyll/index.html

❧ AYRSHIRE

In 1975 Ayrshire became part of the administrative region of Strathclyde. It was established as the county councils of East Ayrshire, North Ayrshire, and South Ayrshire in 1996.

East Ayrshire District History Centre and Baird Institute Museum, Cumnock
http://146.176.15.249/ISC777

North Ayrshire Central Library, Ardrossan
http://146.176.15.249/ISC675

Scottish Maritime Museum, Irvine
http://146.176.15.249/ISC1785

South Ayrshire Central Library, Ayr
http://146.176.15.249/ISC1988.HTM

South Ayrshire Scottish and Local History Library, Ayr
http://www.south-ayrshire.gov.uk/Library/scot_local/Localhistory2.htm

LISTS AND LINKS

✳ Ayrshire GENUKI Home Page
http://home.clara.net/iainkerr/genuki/AYR/

❧ BANFFSHIRE (see also Aberdeenshire)

In 1975 Banffshire became part of the administrative region of Grampian. In 1996 it was established as part of the county council of Aberdeenshire.

Aberdeenshire County Council
http://www.aberdeenshire.gov.uk/

Serves parts of the old counties of Aberdeenshire, Banffshire, and Kincardineshire.

Aberdeen N.E. Scotland Family History Society
http://www.rsc.co.uk/anesfhs/
> Serves the old counties of Aberdeenshire, Banffshire, Kincardineshire, and Morayshire.

Banff Library, Local Studies Collection, Banff
http://146.176.15.249/ISC718

LISTS AND LINKS

※ Banffshire GENUKI Home Page
http://www-theory.dcs.st-and.ac.uk/~mnd/genuki/BAN/

❧ BERWICKSHIRE

> In 1975 Berwickshire became part of the administrative region of The Borders, which in turn was established as the county council of The Scottish Borders in 1996.

Scottish Borders Archive and Local History Centre, Selkirk (Selkirkshire)
http://www.earl.org.uk/familia/services/borders.html
> Serves the Scottish Border counties of Berwickshire, Peeblesshire, Roxburghshire, and Selkirkshire.

Borders Family History Society, Galashiels (Selkirkshire)
http://www.users.zetnet.co.uk/vdunstan/genuki/misc/bordersFHS.html

Duns Library, Duns
http://146.176.15.249/ISC815

INFORMATION SITES

Bibliography of Berwickshire Directories
http://www.users.zetnet.co.uk/vdunstan/genuki/BWK/directories.html

LISTS AND LINKS

※ Berwickshire GENUKI Home Page
http://www.users.zetnet.co.uk/vdunstan/genuki/BWK/

❧ BUTESHIRE

In 1975 Buteshire became part of the administrative region of Strathclyde. It was established as the county council of Argyll and Bute in 1996.

Argyll and Bute Local Studies Library and Information Services, Dunoon (Argyll)
http://www.cqm.co.uk/ab_leisure/lib.html

Argyll and Bute Council Museum and Heritage Organisations
http://www.cqm.co.uk/ab_leisure/musher.html

Isle of Arran Heritage Museum, Brodick
http://www.dalriada.co.uk/celtic_pages/heritage.htm

LISTS AND LINKS

✳ Buteshire GENUKI Home Page
http://www-theory.dcs.st-and.ac.uk/~mnd/genuki/counties/bute.html

❧ CAITHNESS-SHIRE (see also Inverness-shire)

In 1975 Caithness-shire became part of the administrative region of The Highlands, which in turn was established as a county council in 1996.

The North Highland Archive, Wick Library, Wick
http://www.highland.gov.uk/cl/publicservices/archivedetails/
    northarchive.htm

The Archive Service holds the official records of The Highland Council and the five counties which preceded the Regional Council: Caithness-shire, Inverness-shire, Nairnshire, Ross & Cromarty, and Sutherland. In addition it is responsible for the records of thirteen burghs within The Highlands. The North Highland Archive holds the records of Caithness County and the burghs of Wick and Thurso.

Caithness General Library, Caithness and Sutherland NHS Trust, Wick
http://146.176.15.249/ISC1249

INFORMATION SITES

The Highland Council Services in Caithness: Ancestor Search
http://www.highland.gov.uk/cx/a-z/caithness/ancestor_search.htm

LISTS AND LINKS

* Caithness-shire GENUKI Home Page
http://www.frayston.demon.co.uk/genuki/cai/

✺ CLACKMANNANSHIRE

In 1975 Clackmannanshire became part of the administrative region of
Central. It was established as the county council of Clackmannanshire in
1996.

Clackmannan District Library, Alloa
http://146.176.15.249/ISC778

LISTS AND LINKS

* Clackmannanshire GENUKI Home Page
http://www.frayston.demon.co.uk/genuki/cai/

✺ DUMBARTONSHIRE (DUNBARTONSHIRE)

In 1975 Dumbartonshire became part of the administrative region of
Strathclyde. It was established as the county councils of East
Dumbartonshire and West Dumbartonshire in 1996.

Dumbarton Library, Local Studies Collection, Dumbarton
http://146.176.15.249/ISC595

Alexandria Heritage Centre, Alexandria Library, Alexandria
http://www.ifb.co.uk/~kinman/arcnlib.html#alexandria

William Patrick Library, Local Studies Collection, Kirkintilloch
http://146.176.15.249/ISC559

LISTS AND LINKS

✳ Dumbartonshire GENUKI Home Page
**http://www-theory.dcs.st-and.ac.uk/~mnd/genuki/counties/
dunbarton.html**

❧ DUMFRIESSHIRE

In 1975 Dumfriesshire became part of the administrative region of Dumfries and Galloway, which in turn was established as a county council in 1996.

Dumfries and Galloway Archive Centre, Dumfries
http://146.176.15.249/ISC447
Serves the old counties of Dumfriesshire, Kirkcudbrightshire, and Wigtownshire.

Dumfries and Galloway Family History Society Research Centre, Dumfries
http://www.users.globalnet.co.uk/~brownfam/dgfhs.html

Wanlockhead Museum Trust, Wanlockhead Miners' Library, Wanlockhead
http://146.176.15.249/ISC1840

INFORMATION SITES

Dumfries and Galloway Museums and Galleries
http://www.dumfriesmuseum.demon.co.uk/
Serves the former counties of Dumfriesshire, Kirkcudbrightshire, and Wigtownshire.

Parishes of Dumfriesshire
http://www.users.globalnet.co.uk/~brownfam/parish_dfs.html

LISTS AND LINKS

✳ Dumfriesshire GENUKI Home Page
http://www.burgoyne.com/pages/djaggi/genuki/county/dumfries.htm

ક EAST LOTHIAN

In 1975 East Lothian became part of the administrative region of Lothian. It was established as the county council of East Lothian in 1996.

East Lothian Libraries Local History Centre, Haddington
http://www.earl.org.uk/partners/eastlothian/local.htm#LOCAL

LISTS AND LINKS

✻ East Lothian GENUKI Home Page
http://www.users.zetnet.co.uk/vdunstan/genuki/ELN/

ક FIFESHIRE

Fife County Council, Glenrothes
http://www.fife.gov.uk/

Fife Central Library, Local Studies Collection, Kirkaldy
http://146.176.15.249/ISC1008

Scottish Fisheries Museum Library, Anstruther
http://146.176.15.249/ISC1779

INFORMATION SITES

Maritime Fife
http://www.st-and.ac.uk/institutes/sims/marfife/index.htm

LISTS AND LINKS

✻ Fifeshire GENUKI Home Page
http://www.sol.co.uk/w/w.owen/genuki/FIF/index.htm

ક INVERNESS-SHIRE

In 1975 Inverness-shire became part of the administrative region of The Highlands, which in turn was established as a county council in 1996.

The Highland Council Highland Archives Service, Inverness Library,
Inverness
**http://www.highland.gov.uk/cl/publicservices/archivedetails/
highlandarchive.htm**
> The Archive Service holds the official records of The Highland Council and
> the five counties which preceded the Regional Council: Caithness-shire,
> Inverness-shire, Nairnshire, Ross & Cromarty, and Sutherland. In addi-
> tion it is responsible for the records of thirteen burghs within The High-
> lands. The North Highland Archive holds the records of Caithness County
> and the burghs of Wick and Thurso (see under Caithness-shire).

✳ Western Isles Council/Comhairle nan Eilean Siar, Stornoway,
Isle of Lewis
http://www.w-isles.gov.uk/
> The Western Isles Council, now known as Comhairle nan Eilean Siar,
> contains parts of the old counties of Inverness-shire and Ross & Cromarty.

Fort William Library, Fort William
**http://www.highland.gov.uk/cl/publicservices/librariesdetails/
fortwilliam.htm**

The Highland Folk Museum, Kingussie
**http://www.highland.gov.uk/cl/publicservices/museumdetails/
kingussie.htm**

Inverness Library, Local Studies Collection, Inverness
**http://www.highland.gov.uk/cl/publicservices/librariesdetails/
inverness.htm**

Inverness Museum, Inverness
**http://www.highland.gov.uk/cl/publicservices/museumdetails/
inverness.htm**

Portree Library, Portree, Isle of Skye
**http://www.highland.gov.uk/cl/publicservices/librariesdetails/
portree.htm**

Queen's Own Highlanders (Regimental Museum of the Highlanders),
Fort George, Ardersier
http://www.rmhnet.com/blackwatch/

Taigh Chearsabhagh Local History Museum and Community Art Centre,
Lochmaddy, North Uist
http://www.taigh-chearsabhagh.org/

West Highland Museum, Fort William
http://146.176.15.249/ISC1843

The Whyte Photographic Archive, Inverness
**http://www.highland.gov.uk/cl/publicservices/archivedetails/
    whytearchive.htm**
The Whyte Collection forms a major element of the photographic archive
operated by The Highland Council.

INFORMATION SITES

The Highland Council Services in Badenoch and Strathspey, Ancestor
    Search
http://www.highland.gov.uk/cx/a-z/b&s/ancestor_search.htm

The Highland Council Services in Inverness, Ancestor Search
http://www.highland.gov.uk/cx/a-z/inverness/ancestor_search.htm

The Highland Council Services in Lochaber, Ancestor Search
http://www.highland.gov.uk/cx/a-z/lochaber/ancestor_search.htm

The Highland Council Services in Skye and Lochalsh, Ancestor Search
http://www.highland.gov.uk/cx/a-z/s&l/ancestor_search.htm

Highlander Ghosts and Haunted Castles
http://wkweb4.cableinet.co.uk/the.reaper/page1.html

History of Beauly
http://www.cali.co.uk/HIGHEXP/Beauly/History.htm

Isle of Skye Encyclopaedia
http://www.skye.co.uk/encyclopaedia.html

SELECTED DOCUMENTS AND INDEXES ONLINE

Map of The Highland Council Area
http://www.highland.gov.uk/cx/a-z/areamap.htm

LISTS AND LINKS

❋ Inverness-shire GENUKI Home Page
http://www.roe.ac.uk/genuki/inv/index.html

☙ KINCARDINESHIRE (see also Aberdeenshire)

In 1975 Kincardineshire became part of the administrative region of Grampian. It was established as part of the county council of Aberdeenshire in 1996.

Aberdeenshire County Council
http://www.aberdeenshire.gov.uk/
Serves parts of the old counties of Aberdeenshire, Banffshire, and Kincardineshire.

Aberdeen N.E. Scotland Family History Society
http://www.rsc.co.uk/anesfhs/
Serves the old counties of Aberdeenshire, Banffshire, Kincardineshire, and Morayshire.

LISTS AND LINKS

❋ Kincardineshire GENUKI Home Page
http://www.btinternet.com/~mmorton/genuki/KCD/

☙ KINROSS-SHIRE (see also Perthshire)

In 1975 Kinross-shire became part of the administrative region of Tayside. It was established as the county council of Perth and Kinross in 1996.

Perth and Kinross Council Web Site
http://www.pkc.gov.uk/

A.K. Bell Library, Perth
http://www.pkc.gov.uk/

Kinross Library, Kinross
http://146.176.15.249/ISC579

LISTS AND LINKS

❋ Kinross-shire GENUKI Home Page
http://www.dgnscrn.demon.co.uk/genuki/KRS/

&a KIRKCUDBRIGHTSHIRE

(see also Dumfriesshire)

In 1975 Kirkcudbrightshire became part of the administrative region of Dumfries and Galloway, which in turn was established as a county council in 1996.

Dumfries and Galloway Archive Centre, Dumfries
http://146.176.15.249/ISC447
Serves the old counties of Dumfriesshire, Kirkcudbrightshire, and Wigtownshire.

Carsphairn Heritage Centre
http://www.dumfriesmuseum.demon.co.uk/carsp.html

Kirkcudbright Library, Sheriff Court House, Kirkcudbright
http://146.176.15.249/ISC457

INFORMATION SITES

Parishes of Kirkcudbrightshire
http://www.users.globalnet.co.uk/~brownfam/parish_kkd.html

LISTS AND LINKS

* Kirkcudbrightshire GENUKI Home Page
http://www.burgoyne.com/pages/djaggi/genuki/kirkcudb.htm

&a LANARKSHIRE

In 1975 Lanarkskhire became part of the administrative region of Strathclyde. It was established as the county councils of North Lanarkshire and South Lanarkshire in 1996, with a separate city council for the City of Glasgow.

Baillieston Library, Local Studies Collection, Baillieston
http://146.176.15.249/ISC349

Glasgow City Archives, The Mitchell Library, Glasgow
http://146.176.15.249/ISC336

Glasgow University Archives and Business Records Centre
http://www.archives.gla.ac.uk/

74

Lanark Library, Lanark
http://146.176.15.249/ISC653

Leadhills Heritage Trust, Leadhills Miners Library, Biggar
http://146.176.15.249/ISC1695

Mitchell Library, History and Glasgow Room, Glasgow
http://146.176.15.249/ISC339

North Lanarkshire Council, Local Studies Library, Coatbridge
http://146.176.15.249/ISC865

South Lanarkshire Central Library, Local History Studies, Hamilton
http://146.176.15.249/ISC654

INFORMATION SITES

Glasgow University Archives and Business Records Centre Subject
    Source Lists
http://www.archives.gla.ac.uk/arcbrc/resource/lists/default.html

Hyndland Local History Web Site
http://www.hyndl.demon.co.uk/hyndland/0mainindex.htm

LISTS AND LINKS

❋ Lanarkshire GENUKI Home Page
http://www.users.zetnet.co.uk/rdixon/genuki/LKS/index.htm

❧ MIDLOTHIAN

In 1975 Midlothian became part of the administrative regions of The Borders and of Lothian. It was established as the county council of Midlothian in 1996, with a separate city council for the City of Edinburgh.

❋ Midlothian Local Studies Centre and Council Archives, Loanhead
http://www.earl.org.uk/partners/midlothian/local.html

Edinburgh City Central Library, Local Studies Collection
http://146.176.15.249/ISC387

Edinburgh University Library
http://datalib.ed.ac.uk/projects/scimss/

Piershill Library, Local Studies Collection, Edinburgh
http://www.efr.hw.ac.uk/EDC/CapInfo/library.htm#piershill

INFORMATION SITES

Midlothian Monumental Inscriptions
http://freespace.virgin.net/k.young/Monumental%20Inscriptions.htm

LISTS AND LINKS

✳ Midlothian GENUKI Home Page
http://www.btinternet.com/~mmgene/genuki/mln/mlothian.htm

❧ MORAYSHIRE

In 1975 Morayshire became part of the administrative regions of The Highlands and of Grampian. It was established as the separate county council of Moray in 1996.

Moray Council Local Heritage Services, Elgin
http://www.moray.org/techleis/heritage_serv.html

Aberdeen N.E. Scotland Family History Society
http://www.rsc.co.uk/anesfhs/
    Serves the old counties of Aberdeenshire, Banffshire, Kincardineshire, and Morayshire.

INFORMATION SITES

Moray Council Museums Pages
http://www.moray.org/museums/homepage.htm

LISTS AND LINKS

✳ Morayshire GENUKI Home Page
http://www-theory.dcs.st-and.ac.uk/~mnd/genuki/counties/moray.html

❧ NAIRNSHIRE (see also Inverness-shire)

In 1975 Nairnshire became part of the administrative region of The Highlands, which in turn was established as a county council in 1996.

The Highland Council Highland Archives Service, Inverness Library, Inverness
http://www.highland.gov.uk/cl/publicservices/archivedetails/ highlandarchive.htm
> The Archive Service holds the official records of The Highland Council, and the five counties which preceded the Regional Council: Caithness-shire, Inverness-shire, Nairnshire, Ross & Cromarty, and Sutherland. In addition it is responsible for the records of thirteen burghs within The Highlands.

Inverness Library, Local Studies Collection, Inverness
http://www.highland.gov.uk/cl/publicservices/librariesdetails/ inverness.htm

Nairn Fishertown Museum, Nairn
http://www.cali.co.uk/HIGHEXP/Nairn/Fishtown.htm

Nairn Library, Local Studies Collection, Nairn
http://146.176.15.249/ISC1247

Nairn Museum, Viewfield House, Nairn
http://www.highland.gov.uk/cl/publicservices/museumdetails/ nairn.htm

INFORMATION SITES

✳ Town of Nairn History and Background
http://www.cali.co.uk/HIGHEXP/Nairn/Histback.htm

LISTS AND LINKS

✳ Nairnshire GENUKI Home Page
http://www.geocities.com/~brooms/genuki/

❧ ORKNEY

Orkney Islands Council, Kirkwall
http://www.orkney.com/community/index.htm

Orkney FHS, Kirkwall
http://www.tiac.net/users/teschek/genuki/OKI/ofhs.htm

Orkney Museum, Kirkwall
http://www.orkney.com/museums/tankhouse.htm

Stromness Museum, Stromness
http://www.orknet.co.uk/stromnessmuseum/index.htm

INFORMATION SITES

History of the Island of Sanday
http://www.orknet.co.uk/sanday/hist.htm

Orcadian Heritage, Tradition, and Culture
http://www.orkney.com/tradition/index.htm

Sanday Family Names and Connections
http://www.cursiter.com/

LISTS AND LINKS

✻ Orkney GENUKI Home Page
http://www.tiac.net/users/teschek/genuki/OKI/

❧ PEEBLESSHIRE

In 1975 Peeblesshire became part of the administrative region of The Borders, which in turn was established as the county council of The Scottish Borders in 1996.

Scottish Borders Archive and Local History Centre, Selkirk (Selkirkshire)
http://www.earl.org.uk/familia/services/borders.html
Serves the Scottish Border counties of Berwickshire, Peeblesshire, Roxburghshire, and Selkirkshire.

Borders Family History Society, Galashiels (Selkirkshire)
http://www.users.zetnet.co.uk/vdunstan/genuki/misc/bordersFHS.html

Peebles Library, Local Studies Collection, Peebles
http://146.176.15.249/ISC831

LISTS AND LINKS

✻ Peebleshire GENUKI Home Page
http://www.users.zetnet.co.uk/vdunstan/genuki/PEE/

⫸ PERTHSHIRE

In 1975 Perthshire became part of the administrative regions of Central and of Tayside. It was established as the county council of Perth and Kinross in 1996.

Perth and Kinross Council Web Site
http://www.pkc.gov.uk/

A.K. Bell Library, Perth
http://www.earl.org.uk/familia/services/perth_kinross.html

Tayside A Maritime History
http://www.dmcsoft.com/tamh/
Covers the former administrative region of Tayside, including the area of Highland Perthshire, down through Perth to its estuary at Dundee, and parts of Aberdeenshire, Fifeshire, and Kincardineshire.

INFORMATION SITES

Guide to Perthshire
http://www.perth.org.uk/

Perthshire Attractions (museums, libraries, etc.)
http://www.perth.org.uk/html/attrlocn.htm

LISTS AND LINKS

✳ Perthshire GENUKI Home Page
http://www.dundee.ac.uk/~gbuttars/genuki/PER/PER.htm

⫸ RENFREWSHIRE

In 1975 Renfrewshire became part of the administrative region of Strathclyde. It was established as parts of the county councils of East Renfrewshire, Inverclyde, and Renfrewshire in 1996.

Giffnock Community Library, Local Studies Collection, Giffnock, Glasgow
http://www.eastrenfrewshire.gov.uk/community_librarygi.htm# LocalHistory

Inverclyde Council Archives, Watt Library, Greenock
http://146.176.15.249/ISC482

Paisley Central Library, Local Studies Collection, Paisley
http://146.176.15.249/ISC838

SELECTED DOCUMENTS AND INDEXES ONLINE

Pigot's and Slater's Topography of the British Isles: Cathcart
http://www.staffs.ac.uk/schools/humanities_and_soc_sciences/census/
    pigstart.htm

LISTS AND LINKS

✳ Renfrewshire GENUKI Home Page
http://www.skylinc.net/~lasmith/genuki/RFW/

✪ ROSS & CROMARTY
(see also Inverness-shire)

Ross & Cromarty became part of the administrative regions of The Highlands and of the Western Isles in 1975, which in turn became the county
councils in 1996. The Western Isles Council is now known as Comhairle
nan Eilean Siar.

The Highland Council Highland Archives Service, Inverness Library,
    Inverness
http://www.highland.gov.uk/cl/publicservices/archivedetails/
    highlandarchive.htm
The Archive Service holds the official records of The Highland Council,
and the five counties which preceded the Regional Council: Caithness-
shire, Inverness-shire, Nairnshire, Ross & Cromarty, and Sutherland. In
addition it is responsible for the records of thirteen burghs within The
Highlands.

✳ Western Isles Council/Comhairle nan Eilean Siar, Stornoway,
    Isle of Lewis
http://www.w-isles.gov.uk/
The Western Isles Council—now known as Comhairle nan Eilean Siar—is
divided geographically between the counties of Ross & Cromarty (Lewis)
and Inverness-shire (Harris, North and South Uist, Benbecula, and Barra;
Skye and the smaller islands).

Cromarty Courthouse Museum of Cromarty
http://www.cali.co.uk/HIGHEXP/Cromarty/Crthouse.htm

Cromarty Library, Cromarty
**http://www.highland.gov.uk/cl/publicservices/librariesdetails/
cromarty.htm**

Inverness Library, Local Studies Collection, Inverness
**http://www.highland.gov.uk/cl/publicservices/librariesdetails/
inverness.htm**

Kyle of Lochalsh Library, Kyle of Lochalsh
http://146.176.15.249/ISC1272

Museum nan Eilean, Stornoway, Isle of Lewis
http://www.w-isles.gov.uk/museum.htm

INFORMATION SITES

About Ross & Cromarty
http://www.cali.co.uk/HIGHEXP/Rosscrom.htm

Family Tree Research in the Outer Hebrides of Scotland
http://www.hebrides.com/busi/coleis/

The Highland Council Services in Skye and Lochalsh, Ancestor Search
http://www.highland.gov.uk/cx/a-z/s&l/ancestor_search.htm

The Highland Council Services in Ross & Cromarty, Ancestor Search
http://www.highland.gov.uk/cx/a-z/r&c/ancestor_search.htm

The Town of Cromarty and the Past
http://www.cali.co.uk/HIGHEXP/Cromarty/Thepast.htm

Virtual Hebrides/Trusadh nah Eilean
http://www.hebrides.com/new.htm

✳ Western Islands Resource Page, GenWeb Project
http://homepages.rootsweb.com/~cheps/Lewis/index.htm
> The Western Isles include over 200 islands off the Western coast of Scotland and are known as the Outer Hebrides or Outer Isles. The major islands are: Barra (Barraigh), Benbecula (Beinn na Faoghla), Isle of Harris (Na Hearadh), Isle of Lewis (Leodhas), North Uist (Uibhist a Tuath) and South Uist (Uibhist a Deas).

SELECTED DOCUMENTS AND INDEXES ONLINE

Dalriada Archives: The Western Isles
http://www.dalriada.co.uk/archives/isles.htm
> The Archives contain files on the following Isles: Arran, Barra, Benbecula,
> Bute, Harris, Iona, Islay, Lewis, Lismore, Mull, Nthuist (North Uist), Skye,
> and Sthuist (South Uist).

LISTS AND LINKS

✻ Ross & Cromarty GENUKI Home Page
http://www.roe.ac.uk/genuki/roc/index.html

✌ ROXBURGHSHIRE

> In 1975 Roxburghshire became part of the administrative region of The
> Borders, which in turn was established as the county council of The
> Scottish Borders in 1996.

Scottish Borders Archive and Local History Centre, Selkirk (Selkirkshire)
http://www.earl.org.uk/familia/services/borders.html
> Serves the Scottish Border counties of Berwickshire, Peeblesshire,
> Roxburghshire, and Selkirkshire.

Borders Family History Society, Galashiels (Selkirkshire)
http://www.users.zetnet.co.uk/vdunstan/genuki/misc/bordersFHS.html

Hawick Library, Hawick
http://146.176.15.249/ISC822

INFORMATION SITES

Bibliography of Roxburghshire Directories
http://www.users.zetnet.co.uk/vdunstan/genuki/ROX/directories.html

History of Denholm Village
http://www.theshambles.freeserve.co.uk/den1.htm

History of Melrose
http://www.melrose.bordernet.co.uk/history/index.htm

Town of Jedburgh Traditions and Genealogy
http://www.scottishborders.com/web/jedburgh/traditions4.html

Town Yetholm in the Days of the Village Herd
http://www.scottishborders.com/web/yetholm/yet4.html

LISTS AND LINKS

✳ Roxburghshire GENUKI Home Page
http://www.users.zetnet.co.uk/vdunstan/genuki/ROX/

❧ SELKIRKSHIRE

In 1975 Selkirkshire became part of the administrative region of The Borders, which in turn was established as the county council of The Scottish Borders in 1996.

Scottish Borders Archive and Local History Centre, Selkirk
http://www.earl.org.uk/familia/services/borders.html
Serves the Scottish Border counties of Berwickshire, Peeblesshire, Roxburghshire, and Selkirkshire.

Borders Family History Society, Galashiels
http://www.users.zetnet.co.uk/vdunstan/genuki/misc/bordersFHS.html

Galashiels Library, Galashiels
http://146.176.15.249/ISC820

Selkirk Library, Local Studies Collection, Selkirk
http://146.176.15.249/ISC833

INFORMATION SITES

Bibliography of Selkirkshire Directories
http://www.users.zetnet.co.uk/vdunstan/genuki/SEL/directories.html

LISTS AND LINKS

✳ Selkirkshire GENUKI Home Page
http://www.users.zetnet.co.uk/vdunstan/genuki/SEL/

❧ SHETLAND

Shetland Islands Council, Lerwick
http://www.shetland.gov.uk/

Shetland Museums Service
http://www.shetland-museum.org.uk/

INFORMATION SITES

Shetland Museum Collections
http://www.shetland-museum.org.uk/museum/

The Shetland News (local online newspaper)
http://www.shetland-news.co.uk/

Views of Lerwick
http://www.uhi.ac.uk/shetland/views.htm

LISTS AND LINKS

✻ Shetland GENUKI Home Page
http://www-theory.dcs.st-and.ac.uk/~mnd/genuki/counties/
   shetland.html

❧ STIRLINGSHIRE

In 1975 Stirlingshire became part of the administrative region of Central. It was established as the county council of Stirling in 1996.

Stirling Council Archives Services, Stirling
http://146.176.15.249/ISC1823

Stirling Central Library, Local Studies Collection, Stirling
http://146.176.15.249/ISC634

Falkirk Council Archives, Falkirk Museums History Research Centre, Falkirk
http://www.falkirkmuseums.demon.co.uk/

INFORMATION SITES

History of Falkirk
http://www.electricscotland.com/webclans/septs.htm

History of The Isle of Lismore
http://web.ukonline.co.uk/tom.paterson/lismore.htm#TOP

SELECTED DOCUMENTS AND INDEXES ONLINE

Stirlingshire Map, 1841, West Parishes
http://web.ukonline.co.uk/tom.paterson/places/mapstirl00.htm

LISTS AND LINKS

Stirling Library List
http://www.st-and.ac.uk/institutes/sims/marfife/index.htm

✳ Stirlingshire GENUKI Home Page
http://www-theory.dcs.st-and.ac.uk/~mnd/genuki/counties/stirling.html

❧ SUTHERLAND (see also Caithness-shire and Inverness-shire)

In 1975 Sutherland became part of the administrative region of The Highlands, which in turn was established as a county council in 1996.

The Highland Council Highland Archives Service, Inverness Library, Inverness
http://www.highland.gov.uk/cl/publicservices/archivedetails/ highlandarchive.htm
The Archive Service holds the official records of The Highland Council and the five counties which preceded the Regional Council: Caithness-shire, Inverness-shire, Nairnshire, Ross & Cromarty, and Sutherland. In addition it is responsible for the records of thirteen burghs within The Highlands. The North Highland Archive holds the records of Caithness County and the burghs of Wick and Thurso (see under Caithness-shire).

Caithness General Library, Caithness and Sutherland NHS Trust, Wick
http://146.176.15.249/ISC1249

Dornoch Library, Local History Collection, Dornoch
http://www.highland.gov.uk/cl/publicservices/librariesdetails/ dornoch.htm

INFORMATION SITES

The Highland Council Services in Sutherland: Local History
http://www.highland.gov.uk/cx/a-z/sutherland/local_history- information.htm

LISTS AND LINKS

✳ Sutherland GENUKI Home Page
http://www-theory.dcs.st-and.ac.uk/~mnd/genuki/counties/
    sutherland.html

❧ WEST LOTHIAN

In 1975 West Lothian became part of the administrative regions of Central and of of Lothian. It was established as the county council of West Lothian in 1996.

West Lothian Council Archives, Livingston
http://www.westlothian.gov.uk/libraries/archives.htm

Holdings include minutes of the old burgh and community councils, pre-1855 Old Parish Registers for West Lothian, etc.

West Lothian Local History Library, Blackburn
http://www.westlothian.gov.uk/libraries/local.htm

LISTS AND LINKS

✳ West Lothian GENUKI Home Page
http://www-theory.dcs.st-and.ac.uk/~mnd/genuki/WLN/index.html

❧ WIGTOWNSHIRE (see also Dumfriesshire)

In 1975 Wigtownshire became part of the administrative region of Dumfries and Galloway, which in turn was established as a county council in 1996.

Dumfries and Galloway Archive Centre, Dumfries
http://146.176.15.249/ISC447
Serves the old counties of Dumfriesshire, Kirkcudbrightshire, and Wigtownshire.

Wigtown Library, Local Studies Collection, Wigtown
http://146.176.15.249/ISC469

INFORMATION SITES

Parishes of Wigtownshire
http://www.users.globalnet.co.uk/~brownfam/parish_wig.html

SELECTED DOCUMENTS AND INDEXES ONLINE

Pigot's and Slater's Topography of the British Isles: Wigtownshire
**http://www.staffs.ac.uk/schools/humanities_and_soc_sciences/census/
pigstart.htm**

LISTS AND LINKS

✽ Wigtownshire GENUKI Home Page
http://www.burgoyne.com/pages/djaggi/genuki/county1/wigtown.htm

THE ISLE OF MAN
(dependency of the British Crown)

Centre for Manx Studies/Laare-Studeyrys Manninagh, Douglas
http://www.liv.ac.uk/ManxStudies/

INFORMATION SITES

Gazetteer of the Isle of Man
http://www.ee.surrey.ac.uk/Contrib/manx/gazateer/woods/index.htm

Isle of Man Bibliography
http://www.ee.surrey.ac.uk/Contrib/manx/books/authors.htm

Parishes of the Isle of Man and Their Churches
http://www.ee.surrey.ac.uk/Contrib/manx/parishes/index.htm

SELECTED DOCUMENTS AND INDEXES ONLINE

Isle of Man Family History Society Journal, Vols. 1–18
http://www.ee.surrey.ac.uk/Contrib/manx/famhist/fhsjidx.htm

❋ *A Manx Note Book: An Electronic Compendium of Matters Past and Present Connected with the Isle of Man*, ed. by Frances Coakley
http://www.ee.surrey.ac.uk/Contrib/manx/index.htm

Manx Memory: Electronic Resources for Manx Studies/Cooinaghtyn Manninagh: Stoo Lectraneagh son Studeyryssyn Manninagh
http://www.smo.uhi.ac.uk/~stephen/manxmemorywww.html

Map of the Isle of Man, 1724
http://www.rsl.ox.ac.uk/nnj/iom.gif

Witchcraft in Mann, 1712–1713
http://www.smo.uhi.ac.uk/~stephen/1713.pdf
  Transcript of trial source material relating to the examination and trial for witchcraft and sorcery of Alice Cowley and Isabel Gawne.

LISTS AND LINKS

❋ Isle of Man GENUKI Home Page
http://www.genuki.org.uk/big/Iom.html

❋ Isle of Man GenWeb Project
http://homepages.rootsweb.com/~cheps/IOM/

THE CHANNEL ISLANDS
(dependency of the British Crown)

❋ Channel Islands GENUKI Home Page
http://user.itl.net/~glen/genukici.html

❧ GUERNSEY

States of Guernsey Island Archives Service, St. Peter Port
http://user.itl.net/~glen/archgsy.html

Alderney Society and Museum, High Street, Alderney
http://user.itl.net/~glen/aldmuseum.html

Parish of Castel/Paroisse du Castel
http://www.guernsey.net/~st-matthews/castel/

Priaulx Library, St. Peter Port
http://user.itl.net/~glen/priaulx.html

La Société Guernesiaise, Family History Section, St. Peter Port
http://user.itl.net/~glen/fhssocguer.html

INFORMATION SITES

Alderney Ancestry
http://user.itl.net/~glen/alderney.html

Sark Ancestry
http://user.itl.net/~glen/sark.html

Smaller Islands of the Bailiwick of Guernsey
http://www.guernsey.net/~holiday-g/oisland.html

SELECTED DOCUMENTS AND INDEXES ONLINE

Alderney Commercial Directory (1851)
http://user.itl.net/~glen/aldcomm.html

Division of the Common Lands in Alderney, 1831
http://user.itl.net/~glen/aldcommon.html

Pigot's and Slater's Topography of the British Isles: Sark (from *Kelly's Post Office Directory for 1857*)
http://www.staffs.ac.uk/schools/humanities_and_soc_sciences/census/pigstart.htm

LISTS AND LINKS

✻ Guernsey, Alderney, and Sark GENUKI Home Page
http://user.itl.net/~glen/guernsey.html

୬ JERSEY

Jersey Archives Service, St. Helier
http://www.jersey.gov.uk/jerseyarchives/index.html

Channel Islands FHS, St. Helier
http://user.itl.net/~glen/AboutttheChannelIslandsFHS.html

Jersey Reference Library, St. Helier
http://www.itl.net/vc/europe/jersey/Education/library/ref.html

Société Jersiaise Library, St. Helier
http://www.societe-jersiaise.org/

St. Andrew's Church, St. Helier
http://www.localdial.com/users/mtaylor/

St. Aubin on the Hill
http://www.jerseyisland.com/staubin/hill/

SELECTED DOCUMENTS AND INDEXES ONLINE

Map of Jersey, 1639
http://www.rsl.ox.ac.uk/nnj/webmapsf.htm

LISTS AND LINKS

✽ Jersey GENUKI Home Page
http://user.itl.net/~glen/jersey.html

THE REPUBLIC OF IRELAND AND NORTHERN IRELAND

In 1922 the Irish Free State (which became the Republic of Ireland) was formed from twenty-six of the thirty-two Irish counties. Most of the northern province of Ulster (the counties of Antrim, Armagh, Down, Fermanagh, Londonderry, and Tyrone) remained part of the UK. There is a separate record office in Belfast for Northern Ireland, but materials on the northern counties can also be found at the National Archives in Dublin. There are also records for all of Ireland at the Public Record Office in Kew (see England).

National Archives of Ireland/An Chartlann Náisiúnta, Dublin
http://www.nationalarchives.ie/

National Library of Ireland, Dublin
http://www.heanet.ie/natlib/

Public Record Office of Northern Ireland (PRONI), Belfast
http://proni.nics.gov.uk/index.htm

Garda Síochána Museum and Archives, Dublin
http://www.geocities.com/CapitolHill/7900/museum.html
> Archives of the Republic of Ireland's national police force, with archival material also on the Irish Constabulary, the Royal Irish Constabulary, the Dublin Police, and the Dublin Metropolitan Police.

✳ Irish Family History Foundation
http://www.irish-roots.net/

Ulster Historical Foundation
http://www.uhf.org.uk/

INFORMATION SITES

✳ Browse Ireland: Irish Family Names
http://www.browseireland.com/geneo_fn.htm

Church of Ireland Parish Records: Earliest Dates
http://www.geocities.com/ad_container/pop.html?cuid=10183&
    keywords=none

Family History Research at the National Library of Ireland
http://www.heanet.ie/natlib/family_research.html

Great Famine Sources, 1845–1850
http://www.nationalarchives.ie/famine.html

✳ The Great Irish Famine: An Gorta Môr
http://www.wisc.edu/history/famine/plu.html

Guide to Family History and Genealogy Resources at the National
    Archives of Ireland
http://www.nationalarchives.ie/genealogy.html

History of the Baronies of Ireland
http://www.fortunecity.com/bally/kilkenny/2/baronies.htm

✳ Heritage of Ireland Site
http://www.heritageireland.ie/en/frontpage.html

✳ Irish Clans and Names Search
http://www.clansandnames.org/

✳ Irish History on the Web
http://wwwvms.utexas.edu/~jdana/irehist.html

A List of First Names Commonly Used in Ireland
http://www.hylit.com/info/Names/

"The Myth of the Black Irish"
http://www.hypertext.com/blackirish/

Scotch-Irish Research
http://www.familytreemaker.com/00000384.html

Sources for Women's History at the National Archives of Ireland
http://www.nationalarchives.ie/women.html

✳ Universities with Irish Studies (worldwide)
http://wwwvms.utexas.edu/~jdana/history/irishstudies.html

SELECTED DOCUMENTS AND INDEXES ONLINE

Cholera Map of Ireland, 1848–1850
http://www.wisc.edu/history/famine/cholera.html

Database of Irish Historical Statistics
http://www.qub.ac.uk/ss/csr/iredb/dbhme.htm

Immigrant Ships Transcribers Guild: Irish Ports
http://istg.rootsweb.com/departures/ireland.html
    Ports of Belfast, Derry, Galway, Larne, Limerick, Londonderry, Moville,
    Queenstown, and Tralee.

Introduction to *Slater's Topography of Ireland* (1846), (new illus. ed.) in
    Hypertext, ed. by David Alan Gatley, Staffordshire University, 1998
http://www.staffs.ac.uk/schools/humanities_and_soc_sciences/census/
    tp.htm

Ireland-Australia Transportation Index, 1791–1868
http://www.nationalarchives.ie/search01.html
> Index to entries in the surviving records of convicts and their family members who were transported to Australia.

Irish Emigrants Passenger Lists (searchable)
http://genealogy.org/~ajmorris/ireland/ireemg.htm

✳ Irish History in Maps
http://www.fortunecity.com/bally/kilkenny/2/iremaps.htm

✳ Irish Library Online Public Access Catalogues (OPACs)
http://www.heanet.ie/links/irish/library_opacs.html

The Irish Times Surname History Search
http://www.irish-times.com/ancestor/surname/surnameentry.cfm

Map of Ireland, 1798
http://www.library.yale.edu/MapColl/ire1798.htm

Map of Irish Poor Law Unions, 1842–1849
http://www.wisc.edu/history/famine/plu.html

Ordnance Survey Parish List Search Page
http://www.nationalarchives.ie/cgi-bin/naigenform02?index=OS+
     Parish+List

Scanned Images of Prefaces for the Nineteenth-Century Population
     Censuses of Ireland
http://www.qub.ac.uk/ss/csr/iredb/pages.htm
> Printed reports of the censuses of 1813, 1821, 1841, 1851, 1861, 1871, 1881, 1891, 1901, and 1911. These are not enumerations, which unfortunately were destroyed in 1922.

Ulster Historical Foundation Subscribers' Interests Database
http://www.uhf.org.uk/frames.htm

Ulster Historical Foundation Surnames/Householders Report
http://www.uhf.org.uk/frames.htm
> Gives the frequency of surnames in the parishes and counties in the province of Ulster (Antrim, Armagh, Cavan, Donegal, Down, Fermanagh, Londonderry, Monaghan, and Tyrone).

LISTS AND LINKS

* IHA (*The Irish at Home and Abroad*) Online Links
http://www.ihaonline.com/irishlinks.htm

* Ireland GENUKI Home Page
http://www.cs.ncl.ac.uk/genuki/irl/

* IrelandGenWeb Project
http://www.rootsweb.com/~irlwgw/

* Ireland Public Library Address List
http://ireland.iol.ie/~libcounc/address.htm

* Irish Links from Everything Celtic on the Web
http://celt.net/og/angiris.htm

List of Irish Family History Research Centres
http://ireland.iol.ie/~ohas/page13.html

* Northern Ireland GenWeb Project
http://homepages.rootsweb.com/~cheps/NIR/index.htm

* "Sixty Best Ireland URLs to Know on the Internet"
http://www.geocities.com/Athens/Parthenon/5327/best.htm

ANTRIM

* Ulster Historical Foundation, Belfast: Genealogical Research Service
for the Counties of Antrim and Down
http://www.irish-roots.net/AntmDown.htm

SELECTED DOCUMENTS AND INDEXES ONLINE

Antrim 1851 Census
http://www.genealogy.org/~liam/view.html

Map of Belfast Neighborhoods: Protestant and Catholic
http://www.wisc.edu/history/famine/belfast.html

LISTS AND LINKS

✳ Antrim GENUKI Home Page
http://www.cs.ncl.ac.uk/genuki/irl/Antrim/

❧ ARMAGH

✳ County Armagh Genealogy Centre, Armagh
http://www.irish-roots.net/Armagh.htm

LISTS AND LINKS

✳ Armagh GENUKI Home Page
http://www.cs.ncl.ac.uk/genuki/irl/Armagh/

❧ CARLOW

✳ Carlow Research Centre, Carlow Town
http://www.irish-roots.net/Carlow.htm

LISTS AND LINKS

✳ Carlow GENUKI Home Page
http://www.cs.ncl.ac.uk/genuki/irl/Carlow/

❧ CAVAN

✳ Cavan Research Centre, Cavan
http://www.irish-roots.net/Cavan.htm

LISTS AND LINKS

✳ Cavan GENUKI Home Page
http://www.cs.ncl.ac.uk/genuki/irl/Cavan/

❧ CLARE

✳ Clare Heritage and Genealogical Centre, Corofin
http://www.irish-roots.net/Clare.htm

County Clare Local Studies Centre, Ennis
http://ireland.iol.ie/~clarelib/locstudi.htm

LISTS AND LINKS

✳ Clare GENUKI Home Page
http://www.cs.ncl.ac.uk/genuki/irl/Clare/

❧ CORK

✳ Mallow Heritage Centre, Mallow
http://www.irish-roots.net/Cork.htm

INFORMATION SITES

County Cork Libraries and Historical Societies
http://world.std.com/~ahern/cork.html

The Famine Years in Mallow as Reported in *The Cork Examiner*
http://world.std.com/~ahern/mexam.html

SELECTED DOCUMENTS AND INDEXES ONLINE

Map of Cork, 1590
http://www.library.yale.edu/MapColl/cork.htm

Return of Owners of Land in Mallow, 1876
http://world.std.com/~ahern/mloii.htm

LISTS AND LINKS

✳ Cork GENUKI Home Page
http://www.cs.ncl.ac.uk/genuki/irl/Cork/

❧ DONEGAL

✳ Donegal Ancestry Centre, Ramelton
http://www.irish-roots.net/Donegal.htm

INFORMATION SITES

Tracing Your Clonmany Ancestors, by Godfrey F. Duffy
http://www.clonmany.ie.nu/general/ancestors.htm

LISTS AND LINKS

✳ Donegal GENUKI Home Page
http://www.cs.ncl.ac.uk/genuki/irl/Donegal/

❧ DOWN

✳ Ulster Historical Foundation, Belfast: Genealogical Research Service
  for the Counties of Antrim and Down
http://www.irish-roots.net/AntmDown.htm

LISTS AND LINKS

✳ Down GENUKI Home Page
http://www.cs.ncl.ac.uk/genuki/irl/Down/

❧ DUBLIN

Dublin City Archive
http://www.iol.ie/resource/dublincitylibrary/archives.htm

Dublin City Public Libraries, Dublin and Irish Collections
http://www.iol.ie/resource/dublincitylibrary/index.html

✳ Dun Laoghaire Rathdown Heritage Society, Dun Laoghaire (serves
  South Dublin)
http://www.irish-roots.net/DunLghre.htm

✳ Fingal Heritage Group, Swords (serves North Dublin)
http://www.irish-roots.net/Fingal.htm

Library and Archives of Christ Church Cathedral, Dublin
http://aoife.indigo.ie/~cccdub/archives/archives.html

Marsh's Library, Dublin
http://www.kst.dit.ie/marsh/library.html
> The first public library in Ireland, it has an extensive collection of Irish history and genealogical resources.

INFORMATION SITES

Streets of Dublin
http://www.atlanticisland.ie/atlanticisland/dublin.html

SELECTED DOCUMENTS AND INDEXES ONLINE

Shaw's *Dublin City Directory* (1850)
http://homepage.tinet.ie/~plough/dubdir.html

LISTS AND LINKS

✳ Dublin GENUKI Home Page
http://www.cs.ncl.ac.uk/genuki/irl/Dublin/

❧ FERMANAGH

✳ Heritage World: The Heritage Centre for Fermanagh and Tyrone, Dungannon (County Tyrone)
http://www.irish-roots.net/FnghTyrn.htm

INFORMATION SITES

Bibliography and Resource Listing for County Fermanagh
http://members.aol.com/Manus/nirfermanagh.html

LISTS AND LINKS

✳ Fermanagh GENUKI Home Page
http://www.cs.ncl.ac.uk/genuki/irl/Fermanagh/

❧ GALWAY

Connemara Home Page
http://www.connemara-ireland.com/

✳ East Galway Family History Society, Woodford, Loughrea
http://www.irish-roots.net/EtGalway.htm

✳ West Galway Family History Society, Galway
http://www.irish-roots.net/WtGalway.htm

LISTS AND LINKS

✳ Galway GENUKI Home Page
http://www.cs.ncl.ac.uk/genuki/irl/Galway/

❧ KERRY

✳ Killarney Genealogical Centre, Killarney
http://www.irish-roots.net/Kerry.htm

LISTS AND LINKS

✳ Kerry GENUKI Home Page
http://www.cs.ncl.ac.uk/genuki/irl/Kerry/

❧ KILDARE

County Kildare Library, Local Studies Department, Newbridge
http://kildare.ie/library/library/localstudies.htm

✳ The Kildare Heritage and Genealogy Company, Newbridge
http://www.irish-roots.net/Kildare.htm

INFORMATION SITES

County Kildare Genealogical Sources
http://kildare.ie/library/KildareHeritage/page3.html

The Surnames of County Kildare
http://kildare.ie/library/KildareHeritage/Surnames/index.html

LISTS AND LINKS

✳ Kildare GENUKI Home Page
http://www.cs.ncl.ac.uk/genuki/irl/Kildare/

❧ KILKENNY

✳ Kilkenny Ancestry, Kilkenny City
http://www.irish-roots.net/Kilknny.htm

LISTS AND LINKS

✳ Kilkenny GENUKI Home Page
http://www.cs.ncl.ac.uk/genuki/irl/Kilkenny/

❧ LAOIS (LEIX, QUEENS)

✳ Laois and Offaly Family History Research Centre, Tullamore
   (County Offaly)
http://www.irish-roots.net/LaoisOff.htm

INFORMATION SITES

About Offaly and Laois
http://ireland.iol.ie/~ohas/page4.html

LISTS AND LINKS

✳ Laois GENUKI Home Page
http://www.cs.ncl.ac.uk/genuki/irl/Laois/

❧ LEITRIM

✳ Leitrim Genealogy Centre, County Library, Ballinamore
http://www.irish-roots.net/Leitrim.htm

INFORMATION SITES

Leitrim-Roscommon Map Collection
http://guardian.thecore.com/let_ros/L_R_maps_sm.html

LISTS AND LINKS

✳ Leitrim GENUKI Home Page
http://www.cs.ncl.ac.uk/genuki/irl/Leitrim/

100

?? LIMERICK

* Limerick Regional Archives, Limerick City
http://www.irish-roots.net/Limerick.htm

INFORMATION SITES

County Limerick Surnames and Queries
http://www.geocities.com/Athens/Parthenon/6108/limerick.htm

LISTS AND LINKS

* Limerick GENUKI Home Page
http://www.cs.ncl.ac.uk/genuki/irl/Limerick/

?? LONDONDERRY (DERRY)

* County Derry or Londonderry Genealogy Centre, Derry City
http://www.irish-roots.net/Derry.htm

LISTS AND LINKS

* Londonderry GENUKI Home Page
http://www.cs.ncl.ac.uk/genuki/irl/Derry/

?? LONGFORD

County Longford Library, Local History Collection, Longford
http://longford.local.ie/agencies/local_government/longford_library/
history.shtml

* Longford Research Centre, Longford
http://www.irish-roots.net/Longford.htm

LISTS AND LINKS

* Longford GENUKI Home Page
http://www.cs.ncl.ac.uk/genuki/irl/Longford/

❧ LOUTH

* Meath-Louth Family Research Centre, Trim (County Meath)
http://www.irish-roots.net/Louth.htm

INFORMATION SITES

* County Louth Online Magazine
http://homepage.tinet.ie/~dkerr/

LISTS AND LINKS

* Louth GENUKI Home Page
http://www.cs.ncl.ac.uk/genuki/irl/Louth/

❧ MAYO

* County Mayo Family History Centres, Ballina and Ballinrobe
http://mayo.irish-roots.net/Centres.htm

County Mayo Library Service
http://www.mayo-ireland.ie/Mayo/CoDev/MayoLibs.htm

INFORMATION SITES

Mayo Surnames in Griffith's Primary Valuation
ftp://ftp.genealogy.org/pub/genealogy/vendors/ajmorris/mysurn.txt

LISTS AND LINKS

* Mayo GENUKI Home Page
http://www.cs.ncl.ac.uk/genuki/irl/Mayo/

❧ MEATH

* Meath-Louth Family Research Centre, Trim
http://www.irish-roots.net/Louth.htm

LISTS AND LINKS

* Meath GENUKI Home Page
http://www.cs.ncl.ac.uk/genuki/irl/Meath/

❧ MONAGHAN

❋ Monaghan Ancestry, Clogher Historical Society, Monaghan
http://www.irish-roots.net/Monaghan.htm

LISTS AND LINKS

❋ Monaghan GENUKI Home Page
http://www.cs.ncl.ac.uk/genuki/irl/Monaghan/

❧ OFFALY (KINGS)

❋ Laois and Offaly Family History Research Centre, Tullamore
http://www.irish-roots.net/LaoisOff.htm

INFORMATION SITES

About Offaly and Laois
http://ireland.iol.ie/~ohas/page4.html

Bibliography of County Offaly History
http://ireland.iol.ie/~ohas/page18.html

LISTS AND LINKS

❋ Offaly GENUKI Home Page
http://www.cs.ncl.ac.uk/genuki/irl/Offaly/

❧ ROSCOMMON

❋ County Roscommon Heritage and Genealogy Society, Strokestown
http://www.irish-roots.net/Roscmmn.htm

INFORMATION SITES

Leitrim-Roscommon Map Collection
http://guardian.thecore.com/let_ros/L_R_maps_sm.html

LISTS AND LINKS

❋ Roscommon GENUKI Home Page
http://www.cs.ncl.ac.uk/genuki/irl/Roscommon/

❧ SLIGO

* County Sligo Heritage and Genealogy Centre, Sligo City
http://www.irish-roots.net/Sligo.htm

LISTS AND LINKS

* Sligo GENUKI Home Page
http://www.cs.ncl.ac.uk/genuki/irl/Sligo/

❧ TIPPERARY

* Bru Boru Heritage Centre, Rock of Cashel
http://www.irish-roots.net/STipp.htm

County Tipperary Historical Society/Cumann Staire Chontae Thiobraid
    Árann, Thurles
http://www.iol.ie/~tipplibs/Welcome.htm

Tipperary Libraries, Local Studies Department/Leabharlanna Thiobraid
    Árann, Thurles
http://ireland.iol.ie/~tipplibs/Local.htm#Local

* Tipperary North Family Research Centre, Nenagh
http://www.irish-roots.net/NTipp.htm

LISTS AND LINKS

* Tipperary GENUKI Home Page
http://www.cs.ncl.ac.uk/genuki/irl/Tipperary/

❧ TYRONE

* Heritage World: The Heritage Centre for Fermanagh and Tyrone,
    Dungannon
http://www.irish-roots.net/FnghTyrn.htm

INFORMATION SITES

Church Towns in County Tyrone
http://www.teesee.com/CoTyrone/tyvrtranscriptions/tychurch.htm

County Tyrone Roman Catholic Church Records
http://www.teesee.com/CoTyrone/tyvrtranscriptions/rccrty.htm

County Tyrone Source Lists
http://www.teesee.com/CoTyrone/tyresources/tyrsource.htm

LISTS AND LINKS

✳ Tyrone GENUKI Home Page
http://www.cs.ncl.ac.uk/genuki/irl/Tyrone/

❧ WATERFORD

Dungarvan Museum Society, Dungarvan
http://members.tripod.com/~dungarvan/ymuse.htm

✳ Waterford Heritage Centre, Waterford City
http://www.irish-roots.net/Waterfrd.htm

LISTS AND LINKS

✳ Waterford GENUKI Home Page
http://www.cs.ncl.ac.uk/genuki/irl/Waterford/

❧ WESTMEATH

✳ Dun na Si Heritage Centre, Knockdanney, Moate
http://www.irish-roots.net/Wstmeath.htm

SELECTED DOCUMENTS AND INDEXES ONLINE

Pigot's and Slater's Topography of the British Isles: Westmeath, Athlone
http://www.staffs.ac.uk/schools/humanities_and_soc_sciences/census/
    pigstart.htm

LISTS AND LINKS

✳ Westmeath GENUKI Home Page
http://www.cs.ncl.ac.uk/genuki/irl/Westmeath/

❧ WEXFORD

✴ Wexford Genealogy Centre, Tagoat
http://www.irish-roots.net/Wexford.htm

INFORMATION SITES

Wexford Heritage
http://ireland.iol.ie/~wextour/heritage.htm

LISTS AND LINKS

✴ Wexford GENUKI Home Page
http://www.cs.ncl.ac.uk/genuki/irl/Wexford/

❧ WICKLOW

✴ Wicklow Research Centre (location unknown)
http://www.irish-roots.net/Wicklow.htm

INFORMATION SITES

Wicklow Surnames in Griffith's Primary Valuation
ftp://ftp.genealogy.org/pub/genealogy/vendors/ajmorris/wksurn.txt

LISTS AND LINKS

✴ Wicklow GENUKI Home Page
http://www.cs.ncl.ac.uk/genuki/irl/Wicklow/

CELTIC LANGUAGE AND HISTORY WEB SITES

The Celtic languages can be split into two separate groups:
* **Goidelic** (q-Celtic languages): spoken by the first group of Celtic immigrants to the British Isles (about 2000 to 1200 BC). Their language was related to Italic, the predecessor of Latin. Goidelic led to the development of **Irish, Manx, and Scottish**.
* **Brythonic** (p-Celtic languages): spoken by the second group of Celtic immigrants to the British Isles, a wave of Celts referred to as the p-Celts. The languages of **Breton (spoken in Brittany), Cornish, and Welsh** are all offshoots of Brythonic.

The terms q-Celtic and p-Celtic derive from the spelling, usage, and pronunciation of the letters q and p.

❧ GENERAL INFORMATION

Dalriada Archives: History and Genealogy
http://www.dalriada.co.uk/archives/history.htm

Dalriada Celtic Heritage Trust, Brodick, Isle of Arran, Scotland
http://www.dalriada.co.uk/

The Encyclopaedia of the Celts, by Knud Mariboe
http://www.ealaghol.demon.co.uk/celtenc/celt_ind.htm

✳ Every Celtic Thing on the Web
http://celt.net/og/ething.htm

GAELDICT/Gaelic Text Database. 4th ed. (1998)
http://ceantar.org/Comp/GAELDI98.HTML

✳ Gaelic Dictionaries Online (Manx Gaelic/Gaelg, Irish Gaelic/Gaeilge, and Scottish Gaelic/Gáidhlig)
http://ceantar.org/Dicts/index.html

Map of Celtic Tribes by Location
http://www.cadvision.com/hooker-perron/map.htm

Who Were the Celts?
http://metalab.unc.edu/gaelic/celts.html

❧ CORNISH LANGUAGE RESOURCES

Bards of The Gorsedd of Cornwall in Australia
http://www.ozemail.com.au/~kevrenor/gorseth.html

English-Cornish Lexicon/Gerva Sawsnak-Kernauk
http://www.clas.demon.co.uk/clas2/g-gerva.htm

Introduction to Cornish
http://www.clas.demon.co.uk/clas2/g-raglav.htm

Kowethas an Yeth Kernewek/Cornish Language Fellowship, Liskeard
http://nexus6.robots.eeng.liv.ac.uk/~evansjon/kowethas.htm

Kresenn an Yeth Kernewek/Cornish Language Centre
http://homepages.newnet.co.uk/lindamarriott/kernewek/cornish.html

❧ IRISH LANGUAGE RESOURCES

An Chrannóg (Irish Language College), Donegal
http://members.xoom.com/Crannog/

History of the Gaeltacht
http://www.iol.ie/~obrienp/rathcarn/gaelt_b.htm
> The Gaeltacht covers large parts of counties Donegal, Galway, Kerry, and Mayo and also parts of counties Cork, Meath, and Waterford. These are the only places in Ireland where Irish is still spoken as a community language (English is also spoken).

Old Irish-Gaelic Surnames
http://www.fortunecity.com/bally/kilkenny/2/irenames.htm

Ráleabhear/Irish Phrase Book, by Pádraig Mac Con Uladh
http://members.xoom.com/Druid57/r1.htm

❧ MANX LANGUAGE RESOURCES

Fockleyr Gaelg-Baarle. 3rd ed. (1993) (Manx-English dictionary)
http://www.ceantar.org/Dicts/Manx/index.html

Manx Gaelic Society/Yn Cheshaght Ghailckagh, St. Jude's, Isle of Man
http://www.manxman.co.im/gaelic/mgs/mgs.htm

Manx Language Resources
http://homepages.enterprise.net/kelly/index.html

SCOTTISH LANGUAGE RESOURCES

Cinnidhean: Genealogy
http://www.smo.uhi.ac.uk/cnag/failte/Failte97/f6b.html

Gáidhlig ann an Alba-Eóladair/A Guide to Gaelic Scotland
http://www.smo.uhi.ac.uk/cnag/failte/

Information on the Gaelic Language
http://www.highland.gov.uk/cl/publicservices/gaelic/index.htm

Online Gaelic Lessons
http://www.smo.uhi.ac.uk/beurla/Gaelic_lessons.html

Sabhal Môr Ostaig (a Gaelic studies college), Armadale, Isle of Skye
http://www.smo.uhi.ac.uk/beurla/

The School Gaelic Dictionary, by Malcolm MacFarlane (1912)
http://www.smo.uhi.ac.uk/gaidhlig/faclair/macfarlane

Scots Language Resource Centre
http://www.pkc.gov.uk/slrc/

WELSH LANGUAGE RESOURCES

Cymdeithas yr Iaith Gymraeg/Welsh Language Society
http://www.aber.ac.uk/~cymwww/cyflwyniad.htm

A Welsh Language Course
http://www.cs.brown.edu/fun/welsh/home.html

COUNTY ARCHIVE RESEARCH NETWORK (CARN)

http://www.suffolkcc.gov.uk/libraries_and_heritage/sro/carn.html

The Network consists of the central recording of the names and addresses of visitors using the county record offices and many other local authority record offices in England and Wales. Application forms for reader's tickets are generally available at the search rooms and can be sent by post to correspondents intending to visit a record office. Tickets will normally be valid for four years. A current ticket issued from any of the participating offices or branches will be accepted by all, though actual search room procedures may vary from place to place. Devon, Derbyshire, Dorset, Shropshire, and Warwickshire offices do not issue CARN tickets, but will accept them as proof of identity under their own programs. Sheffield Record Office and Liverpool Central Library Record Office operate separate programs: contact them for details.

⮞ PARTICIPATING OFFICES AND BRANCHES (as of 1998)

Anglesey/Ynys Mon
Berkshire
Birmingham
Buckinghamshire
Bury
Cambridgeshire (offices at Cambridge and Huntingdon)
Ceredigion
Cleveland
Cornwall
Coventry
Cumbria (offices at Barrow, Carlisle, Kendal, and Whitehaven)
Denbighshire
East Sussex
Essex (offices at Chelmsford, Colchester, and Southend)
Flintshire
Greater Manchester
Gwynedd (offices at Caernarfon and Dolgellau)
Gwent
Hampshire

Herefordshire
Hertfordshire
Isle of Wight
Kent (offices at Maidstone, Canterbury, Rochester, Folkestone, Ramsgate, and Sevenoaks)
Lancashire
Leicestershire
Norfolk
Nottinghamshire
Oxfordshire
Portsmouth
Powys
Somerset
Suffolk (offices at Bury St. Edmunds, Ipswich, and Lowestoft)
Surrey
Wiltshire
West Sussex
Wolverhampton
Worcestershire

110

❧ INDEX OF PLACE NAMES